Single to Married

Becoming Who You Are
In Christ and a Better
Complement as a Potential Wife

Chloe M. Gooden

D1445592

Single to Married

Copyright 2013 Chloe M. Gooden

ISBN-13:978-1499633283
ISBN-10:1499633289
Also available in eBook

Cover Design: Diango Lando
Author Photo : Daria L. Blevins

Acknowledgments

To my family who has always been there for me through every trial, blessing, and struggle in my life. I don't know where I would be if God hadn't blessed me with your love and support. Thank you for always being here for me. I love you more than anything.

Love,
Chloe M. Gooden

Introduction

Every girl's dream is to find the men we see in the famous Disney movies and fairy tales. From Cinderella and Rapunzel to Snow White, we have all seen the damsel in distress and her awaited prince rescuing her from misery. Most of all, we enjoy seeing the moment they marry and live happily ever after. We go our whole lives hoping to be found by this fantasy man and think that's the moment our lives will change forever. We have all seen numerous times how the princess's life is at a standstill until she is swept off of her feet by her prince. She is either locked up in a dungeon or living in poverty until the mystery man arrives. The fairy tales and movies always give the impression that she is unable to be or do anything great before her prince has found her. As soon as the prince arrives, her life is magically transformed and she is finally able to have the amazing life she has always dreamed of. We go each day keeping these fairy tales in our minds and prayerfully hoping that this man will find us. We believe our lives are at a standstill until our knight in shining armor arrives.

Unlike the fairy tales, we as women can't just sleep until our mates come and find us. We also cannot be at a standstill until our prince arrives. Many of these stories give the false impression that it takes no effort on the woman's part to find this man; that she doesn't have to do any preparation to be ready for her prince-to-be. These fairy tales are, of course, just that: a fairy tale. It's nice to see the whimsical life of a prince and princess finding each other and experiencing the love they've always waited for. For a moment it gives us hope. It gives us something to hold on to until our one true love has found us. These movies play on our desire to find love and give us a moment of fantasy. They give us a sense of relief that our mate will find us soon and we will be together for a lifetime. Being single, I have found myself loving the same type of movies. I love seeing the woman being courted by her one true love. I love seeing the first moment they meet; the first date; the first moment they touch; their first kiss; the first time they say, "I love you"; the first time they meet each other's parents; and most of all, the moment they realize they can't live another second without each other and decide to marry. It's beautiful, romantic, the sweetest thing you could ever see and also experience. We all are waiting for that moment. Waiting for that guy to look into our eyes and say, "I love you. I can't live without you. Will you marry me?" We dream of this moment all of the time. But has our dreaming held us back from living? Has our dreaming placed us in a daze?

Though it is great to desire a spouse and family, we sometimes tend to dream about it so much that we forget to live in the now; in this moment. God has a purpose for you where you are presently. He isn't sitting in heaven thinking "Okay, soon as she meets Mr. Right, THEN I'll start her life and bless her!" Yes, God bringing you a spouse is one of your blessings, BUT it is not the blessing that is required before other blessings arrive. God has a purpose for you now, and He has so many things you need to fulfill before you meet your mate. He also has much to prepare in you before he arrives. Each day is a blessing from God, whether you are single or married. You have to take joy, regardless of where you are presently, because each day is a gift. Learning how to treat each day as a gift is so vital when waiting for anything we desire from God. We can sometimes find ourselves so focused on where we want to be that we become ungrateful for where God has us now.

Philippians 4:11–13 *"I am not saying this because I am in need, for I have learned to be content whatever the circumstances. I know what it is to be in need, and I know what it is to have plenty. I have learned the secret of being content in any and every situation, whether well fed or hungry, whether living in plenty or in want. I can do all this through him who gives me strength."*

Oftentimes we get in a rut because we treat our situations and present placement as if it is permanent. But the Word tells us differently.

1 Peter 5:10 *"You will have to suffer only a little while; after that, God, who is full of grace, the one who called you to his eternal glory in union with the Messiah, will himself restore, establish and strengthen you and make you firm."*

Any place God has you now is to prepare you for the next step in your life and your purpose. Too often we focus on where we want to be and we miss the blessings He has surrounded us with presently, and we also miss the time to prepare for what He has for us. Don't take for granted where He has you now, whether single or engaged. To everything there is a season; a season to sow and a season to reap. Right now is the perfect time for you to sow into your life and your development as a future wife and mother. You can't truly reap the harvest if you don't properly prepare. This can apply not only to waiting for your spouse but waiting for a desired job, home, and any other desires we are trusting God to give us. I used to do this all the time. Any position I would get, or guy I would date, I would focus so much on where we were going—the end goal—that I couldn't enjoy where I was at that moment. I missed the enjoyment of the newness of a relationship. I missed the innocent dates and nervousness when we talked to each other. I missed feeling that anxiousness and butterflies every time we were supposed to meet. I was trying to rush through the honeymoon phase so I could get to the end goal. For what? Usually out of fear. Usually when we are in a rush to get somewhere, or attain something, it's because we are in fear it will never happen. My fear was controlling me and I was missing all the great things happening around me because I was so focused on the end result. There are probably some great things going on around you right now that you may be missing. Stop right now and for a minute, don't think about what you are reaching for. Don't think about the desires you are waiting to be fulfilled. Don't think about what you wish you had. Don't think about the spouse you are waiting for. Don't think about your wedding day. Stop. I want you to stop and think about what you do have. What things has God already blessed you with? Are you healthy? Do you have people around you that love you? Make a list of the blessings you currently have in your life. I am sure the list can go on and on. You already have blessings overflowing around you; don't miss them. God knows when it is the proper time to bless us with the things we desire and He knows us better than we know ourselves. God cannot give us anything until we are ready and prepared for it. It's like giving a toddler keys to a new Mercedes Benz and tell him to have a go! Though it is a blessing, the child will not understand what he has and it would ultimately be more of a burden then a blessing. He won't know how to use it, treat it, nor will he value it. That's how God is with what He gives us. I know you want love to enter your life, we all do. But can you truly say you are ready?

Table of Contents

Chapter 1

Who Are You?

When you are first born into this world, you aren't sure of who you are until someone tells you. The first moment you realize who you are, you answer by that name and you assume that identity. But what if you didn't know who you were? What if your parents never gave you a name? What if they never told you who your family is, what you come from, and what you can become? You would wander the earth lost. You would answer by any name allowing others to tell you who you are. You would struggle in finding your purpose and possibly never realize the gifts God has placed in you. Why? All because you were never told who you are, nor whose you are.

This is exactly what many of us as Christians are experiencing right now and we don't even realize it. We are wandering this earth not walking in our God-given purpose because we don't know who we are in Christ. We are not mere humans, but God's children: Children of the King. That makes you royalty. When Jesus was on Earth He walked in his purpose because he knew who he was and whose he was. He healed the sick; cast demons into the sea; raised the dead; fed thousands with five loaves of bread and two small fish; and more than anything, died on the cross for our sins. But this is just a snippet of all that He did. With all of the works he performed on this earth He tells us in His Word that we will do even greater works than He.

John 14:12 *"Very truly I tell you, whoever believes in me will do the works I have been doing, and they will do even greater things than these, because I am going to the Father."*

When you truly think about this scripture it's pretty amazing. All that Jesus did on this earth and he says WE will do greater works then he did. Truly meditate on that. If this is true—which we know it is because it is in the Word—shouldn't we be doing the same works Christ did on Earth?

Read these passages. Look at some of the things Jesus did while he was on earth.

Matthew 8:2–3, 5–13–15	John 9
Matthew 9:2–8, 20–22	John 2:1–11
Matthew 20:29–34	John 11:1–45
Mark 7:31–37	John 21:1–11
Mark 8:22–25	John 20:1–31

When you read some of the things Jesus did on Earth, does it amaze you? Does it seem unbelievable? Do you think you can do what Jesus did? I will tell you: you can. But I know you are probably wondering, "Well Chloe, if that's the case, why am I not seeing these things performed on earth?" I'll tell you why. The same reason Jesus told his disciples why they couldn't.

Matthew 17:14–20 *"¹⁴And when they had come to the multitude, a man came to Him, kneeling down to Him and saying, ¹⁵ 'Lord, have mercy on my son, for he is an epileptic and suffers severely; for he often falls into the fire and often into the water. ¹⁶So I brought him to Your disciples, but they could not cure him.' ¹⁷Then Jesus answered and said, "O faithless and perverse generation, how long shall I be with you? How long shall I bear with you? Bring him here to Me.' ¹⁸And Jesus rebuked the demon, and it came out of him; and the child was cured from that very hour. ¹⁹Then the disciples came to Jesus privately and said, 'Why could we not cast it out?' ²⁰So Jesus said to them, 'Because of your unbelief; for assuredly, I say to you, if you have faith as a mustard seed, you will say to this mountain, 'Move from here to there,' and it will move; and* *nothing will be impossible for you.* ²¹*However, this kind does not go out except by prayer and fasting."*

If you notice, when Jesus tells us we will do greater things, and also when he spoke to the disciples, he exclaims that you have to believe to be able to do these great works. He explained to the disciples that it was because of their disbelief that they weren't able to perform the same miracles he did. See, the key to us performing what Jesus did on Earth is that we have to have faith. We have to believe we can do these things and have faith that God has empowered us to do them. That's the key. You have to believe.

Who do you believe you are? What do you think you can do? What do you think you can't do? Why don't you think you can do these things? This is something we need to ask ourselves every day. You are in a lineage of Kings and Queens and you have to know and believe that. You have to believe you have the power of Christ in you and are capable of doing great things. Who has told you differently? What has you thinking you are limited to do something great on this Earth? The world, that's who. Whether because of our color, gender, shape, or because of where we come from, they have placed in our minds that we are limited because of who we are. Also, as stated earlier in the chapter, they have put in our minds that we are nothing if we don't have a mate by our side. Everywhere we go as singles the first thing someone asks, "So when are you going to get married?" Is that the only thing we should be looking forward to in our future? Is that the only thing they see next in us? Yes, it is amazing for your mate to find you and I know when the time is right, he will. But you can amount to great things at ANY point of your life because you already have the perfect mate, the Holy Spirit.

Knowing who you are in Christ is the first step of becoming the woman of God He has called you to be. No matter when your husband finds you, before, or after, you need to know who you are so you won't lose your identity in the relationship. God has gifted you with your own special gifts and the world is waiting for you to execute them! God has amazing plans for your life and He predetermined what you will be and who you are before you were even born.

Jeremiah 29:11 *"For I know the plans I have for you,"*
declares the LORD, *"plans to prosper you and not to harm you,*
plans to give you hope and a future."

He has a predetermined plan for your life. There is something on this earth that you and only you can do! Don't believe your life is at a standstill until your mate finds you. Being a wife and mother is a part of your purpose, but not your ONLY purpose. Understand that. Too many of us get so focused on someone finding us, and we completely forget that we have already been found, by God. God gives us purpose, not our mates. As you are waiting on your Prince Charming to find you, you first need to find out who you are. To do this you have to become focused on the development of yourself physically, mentally, emotionally, and most of all, spiritually.

Right now is not the time to focus only on how you want your spouse to be. How can you know what you need, or the type of man you want, if you don't even know who you are? We get so focused on what we are looking for that we have a specific list for this dreamy man. We know exactly how we want him to look. What type of occupation we prefer. His height, weight, size, everything! We scrutinize this soon coming mate to the T! Now tell me something, how can you scrutinize what your man has to have when you haven't even developed into the full person God has called you to be? We are so quick to point out what we require from our men that we forget to focus on ourselves and become someone that a Godly man wants to be with. Think about it. If you were the man that was every inch of everything you ever dreamed of would you want to date you? Seriously, ask yourself this. Are you ready for what you desire? Would you even complement the man that you wish to come your way? This is the perfect time for you to become that. Not perfect, but the perfect image of what God has called you to be.

Child of a King

To find out who you are you, there are a couple of things you need to know about yourself and where you have come from, your lineage. Not just your earthly lineage, but your spiritual one as well. Your lineage is finding out who your line of descendants are and tracking it to the founding family, person, or race. When looking at our spiritual lineage, it links back to our creator; God.

1 John 3:1 *"Behold, what manner of love the Father hath bestowed upon us, that we should be called the sons of God: therefore the world knoweth us not, because it knew him not.*

1 John 4:4 *"You are of God, little children, and have overcome them, because He who is in you is greater than he who is in the world."*

God calls us His sons and daughters throughout the Bible multiple times. By His grace we have been blessed to be a part of His family with Jesus Christ and the Holy Spirit. When Jesus left to be with God, He sent the Holy Spirit to reside within us. He is our helper. He is the one who cries out to God in our times of trouble and so much more. When we don't have the strength, the knowledge, the words to say to Christ our spirit knows EXACTLY what to say. By being a descendant of Christ, we are imbedded with the same power and gifts as Christ. Therefore, we can do the same works as Christ; but even GREATER works. You can do and be anything because of whom you come from. So let's take a look at some of the things Christ did. As I go through each characteristic, realize that you have this same power within you, and can do these same great works.

Overcomer

1 John 5:4 *"For everyone born of God overcomes the world. This is the victory that has overcome the world, even our faith."*

When God came to this earth in the flesh—Jesus—He came to overcome this world so that we would be able to overcome it as well. By Jesus being here, we have a guaranteed victory over any trial or struggle that comes our way. Jesus had to come in the flesh to experience the same trials and temptations we go through each day on earth. This was done so He could sympathize, comfort us, and show us we can resist anything that comes our way. I love that about God.

5

Instead of just telling us, He decided to come down to earth and SHOW us that anything is possible with Him. No sin on this earth cannot be overcome, period. Jesus gave us that confidence and that same strength is in YOU. So what does that mean for you? Well ask yourself. Is there anything you are struggling with? Maybe it's a sin that you have dealt with for years. Maybe it's an addiction that you can't seem to shake alone? Maybe it's that past mate that keeps popping up in your life that you know isn't good for you? Whatever it may be, you have to ensure to overcome it before your mate comes into your life. Issues that we have not dealt with personally will always come into our relationship if we do not deal with them properly. Being single is the perfect time to stop and work on addictions or habits that need to change. You have the time to be alone with God and truly work on yourself as an individual. Don't forsake this time that He has given you.

Ecclesiastes 3:1 *"To everything there is a season, and a time to every purpose under the heaven..."*

Healer

Throughout Jesus' time on earth He healed many as He traveled throughout many lands. From healing the lame, to bringing those from the dead there are so many illustrations of Jesus showing His compassion to others. I could quote multiple scriptures on the things He did but instead I will let you read these magnificent stories. Simply read Matthew, Mark, Luke, or John. They all give an amazing illustration of Jesus time on earth but are simply written from different perspectives. Jesus did so much in His time here and you can do the same. Everyone has different gifts on earth and have the power of healing in many forms. Your healing may come through your words. You may be an encourager. Your healing may be through your voice. You may be a singer. Or maybe simply just your presence brings healing to others. Whatever form of healing you are able to give; GIVE IT. We all have different gifts but are here for the same purpose; showing love and compassion to others. Don't underestimate the gifts God has given to you. Your gift can heal someone's pain whether it's loneliness or hurt. Think about it. How many times have you been going through something and someone's touch, comforting voice, or encouraging words brought you healing? I'm sure we can all think of at least one situation and the person who gave us that peace. Be that peace for someone else.

Teacher

So I know, of course, when you see teacher, you automatically assume this means you have to be on a stage or in front of a class. But that is not always the case. Jesus taught those not only through His words but also through His actions. Jesus came not only to teach the Word but to show others through His works what God has called us to do and to actually walk in His Word. We all have insight on the Word and are able to teach the Word to others. Some may feel comfortable with speaking God's Word and educating those on the Bible and God's teachings. But they are not the only teachers. You giving to someone in need; that's teaching. You forgiving someone for a wrongdoing; that's teaching. You walking in peace and being that one person who refuses to gossip, that's teaching. Many times the best lessons are taught by what is seen and not heard. Is your walk exemplifying the truth in the Word? Each day we should be exemplifying the light God has put within us and teaching others about God's Word and, most of all, God's love. We should be eager to share it with others we come across. What's funny is that when we've had a good dessert, or have seen an amazing movie we are quick to share it with the first person we see, or the first social media site we can get to. Why not be the same about God?

Forgiver

One of the hardest things for many of us to do is forgive someone; especially if we feel justified in our un-forgiveness. Forgiving someone not only frees the one who has done harm, but it also frees you. This is such an important attribute of Jesus Christ that is possessed in us because it takes away the tendency to judge, critique, and put ourselves above others as though we have never needed grace and mercy. The ability to show forgiveness towards someone is something you truly need to possess to move on to your potential mate and to be prepared for any relationship, especially marriage. I will never forget when I was attending a wedding and, during the tribute speech to the groom, the groomsman's brother said, "Go into the marriage with a fist full of forgiveness." This is so true and imperative in any relationship. We will get offended by someone, it is inevitable. But God repeatedly expresses to us throughout the Word to forgive and to pray for our enemies. Un-forgiveness can grow into bitterness and anger and these two in themselves can ensnare you and keep you from living a life of freedom. Forgiveness is not for the other but for ourselves.

Mark 11:25 *"And when you assume the posture of prayer, remember that it's not all asking. If you have anything against someone, forgive—only then will your heavenly Father be inclined to also wipe your slate clean of sins.*

Matthew 18:21-22 *"21 Then Peter came and said to Him, "Lord, how often shall my brother sin against me and I forgive him? Up to seven times?" 22 Jesus said to him, "I do not say to you, up to seven times, but up to seventy times seven."*

One of the things I love so much about Jesus is that even when He was on the cross and his enemies were in the act of doing Him harm, he showed love and compassion towards them and cried out to God for their forgiveness. Jesus expressed to God, *"Forgive them Lord, for they know not what they do"* Luke 23:24. That is purely amazing to me. God had so much mercy and grace for His people that He cried out for them in the midst of their harm towards Him. If He can do it, we can do it as well, for we are manifested in His image and can do the same works. Practice this in your life in all areas. You will be surprised how much healing you can give to others through forgiveness, and also how much it will heal you.

Lover of All

Jesus was the true example of showing love to all mankind, regardless of who they were or where they came from. Showing love to purpose and who is a distraction. Make pleasing God your focus and desire each day; not finding a man.

Chapter 2

Are You Mrs. Right?

While waiting for our prince we tend to fantasize about him day in and day out. We think about how our lives will be different and how life will become everything we could ever imagine. We have in mind how tall we want him to be; how muscular we want him to be; what type of job we want him to have; what color eyes we hope he has; his style of dress; the type of car we hope he drives; how many degrees he must have; what occupation we hope he has; where he lives; where we hope he is from. The list can go on and on. We have him pretty much summed up in every single detail. But while doing all of this fantasizing, are you trying to become a better you? Do you think you are truly ready to meet this prince you are fantasizing about? For most of us, the answer is, "Probably not." We always think we are ready for a relationship and for this dream guy to sweep us off our feet, but in actuality many of us aren't even close. The reason I say that is because we haven't done anything to prepare for a future mate and have the slight idea of what it means to even be a helpmate. The world has placed in our minds that being prepared for a mate has to do with a physical aspect of preparation and not internal. Think about all the magazines and books out there that say, *"Lose 30 lbs and get the man you want!", "Make your lips fuller and have sexy lips like Angelina Jolie."* We see things like this all the time and they have placed in our minds that if we wear the best clothes, have on the prettiest make up, have the nicest body that we will find love and have a relationship that will last a lifetime. The Bible tells us that physical beauty should not be our focus.

1 Timothy 2:9–10 *"⁹Likewise also that women should adorn themselves in respectable apparel, with modesty and self-control, not with braided hair and gold or pearls or costly attire, ¹⁰but with what is proper for women who profess godliness—with good works."*

1 Peter 3:4 *"But let your adorning be the hidden person of the heart with the imperishable beauty of a gentle and quiet spirit, which in god's sight is very precious."*

Proverbs 31:29 *"Charm is deceptive, and beauty is fleeting; but a woman who fears the lord is to be praised."*

Now in no way am I exclaiming that God sees wearing nice clothes, staying in shape, or wearing jewelry as a sin. What the scripture is trying to stress is that the external beauty is not what matters when it comes to becoming a woman that fears the Lord. Physical beauty has nothing to do with the development of spirit and becoming the woman God has called us to be. It's the *act* of developing of our spirits, character, and relationship with God; truly developing ourselves to be ministers of God, wives, mothers, and all God has called and designed us to be.

I am pretty sure you have heard of the scripture *Proverbs 31*. This is a popular excerpt that is used quite often to describe the idea of a virtuous woman. Let's go through this excerpt and reveal truly what God sees as a virtuous woman. As you read through the scripture, ask yourself, "Am I truly ready to be this woman?"

Proverbs 31:10–11 *"A wife of noble character, who can find? She is worth far more than rubies. Her husband has full confidence in her and lacks nothing of value."*

Being a noble wife involves holding high moral principles and fine personal qualities within yourself and not only acting in this way but truly believing it in your heart. It's ironic the excerpt questions where can you find this type of woman, as if it is rare. Honestly, in this day and age, it is very rare. Look around you. Look on the reality TV shows that exude women showing their bodies, disrespecting each other and their spouses, completely acting in ways that I know are not pleasing in God's eyes. Or just look around you as you go out. Many of us pride ourselves on conforming to the world and its fashions and way of acting instead of referring and conforming to what the Bible entails. We have found it to be normal for us to live the world's way because it is what we see every day. I even find myself conforming to the world's way if I don't stay close to the Word and consistently reminded daily of what God wants and not what the world asks of me. The type of woman that God values has nothing to do with what the world tells us to focus on. He even states that this woman is worth more than rubies. That her worth, her price, is far beyond the richest materials on earth. When a woman walks with value and honor, her husband has FULL confidence in her because he knows that she will act in a noble character and also make decisions that are noble. He doesn't have to wonder how she will act when he is away. He doesn't have to worry that she will not know how to represent the family well. He trusts her judgment and knows he has a woman of value. A woman of honor. Royalty. Do you possess this quality? Are you walking as a noble woman now? Think about the things you do and say each day. Think about how you handle disputes with others, how you carry yourself publicly, how you treat others each day. Are you exemplifying someone of noble character?

Proverbs 31:12–13 *"She brings him good, not harm, all the days of her life. 13 she selects wool and flax and works with eager hands."*

A wife is the woman that the husband seeks to depend on after God. She is expected to be his support, his backbone, the one he can go to and trust with the most vulnerable parts of himself. Trusting her means that she doesn't use his vulnerabilities as a tool to offend him in arguments or disputes; that he can truly come to his wife as a best friend, a support like none other when the entire world is against him. He trusts her because she loves him and he expects her to do him no harm. If you take a look at a lot of reality TV shows you will see wives disrespecting their husbands behind their backs and going against what they have decided as a household because of worldly pressures. It is always so important to keep your business at home and only at home. Now I am not saying you shouldn't seek Godly counsel when issues arise, but don't use gossip about your home and spouse as a way to hurt or harm him. The most important factor in a relationship, besides God, is trust and communication. If you do not trust each other, it will cause a lot of distress and miscommunication in the home and will begin a whirlwind of other issues. Don't base how you treat your husband on what you see around you. When the time comes for you to be married, you will be one with this man. You should treat him just the way you would want to be treated. When you harm him, you are harming yourself and your home. Now, of course, when it comes to the pretext of selecting wool and flax, you have to relate this to our present times and what that means for our generation. In this verse, He is trying to portray that she clothes her children and family and ensures they have what they need to care for them. I love the part about her working with eager hands. This is stating that she is excited, thrilled, and glad to do what is needed to provide and care for her family. She doesn't complain about her job. She doesn't nag about having to care for them; it is her joy. We all have seen how different it is when someone does something but does it as more of a duty then as a pleasure. They have an attitude about doing the job and they make sure everyone knows. No one likes being around that—no one. When someone does something purely because they enjoy it, it shows in their actions and they are a pleasure to be around. A virtuous woman delights in taking care of her family and exudes joy and pleasure in doing so.

Proverbs 31: 14–15 *"She is like the merchant ships, bringing her food from afar. She gets up while it is still night; she provides food for her family and portions for her female servants."*

Once again, this is providing an example of the importance of the woman providing for her family. What's great is it shows not only her love for her family, but also her servants. That she makes sure her entire household is fed and provided for. This is a great example of her hospitality not only to her own family but to those in her vicinity and community. A great portion of taking care of the household is preparation. It exclaims that she gets up while it is still night to prepare for the next day at end. This preparation is so important because her part in taking care of the household is vital for peaceful flow of the next day. Now you and your spouse can decide what that flow looks like. Maybe he helps as well, it is no one person's specific duty; but whatever the part may be that you hold, it is vital to keep the home at peace. I know in my own life that sometimes I don't even feel like preparing for myself, let alone someone else. Are you? A lot of us have gotten used to being alone and we can do things at our own pace because it only affects us. But that changes with a spouse and requires adjustment in our normal day-to-day routine. Are you ready to make adjustments for a spouse and family?

Proverbs 31:16–19 *" She considers a field and buys it; out of her earnings she plants a vineyard. She sets about her work vigorously; her arms are strong for her tasks. She sees that her trading is profitable, and her lamp does not go out at night. In her hand she holds the distaff and grasps the spindle with her fingers. "*

This woman is a hard worker! Though her husband is out providing for the family, she is still doing her part as well in laboring and taking care of home. Whether it involves her working in her own career or as a stay-at-home mom, the wife has her part in laboring for the family as well and the two have to decide on the duties of each other and what works best for them. Also, she handles their finances well and handles the business of the home with wisdom just as her husband does. I thought this was such a great find because many of us independently do not handle our finances well. Or we handle them well, but are used to only having to consider ourselves and no one else. A good wife is wise in finances and does what she can to stretch the finances of the home. To be a partner with her husband and ensure that everyone is well provided for. This reminds me of a verse in the Bible that proclaims the importance of storing up wealth for your future generations; that we should build an inheritance for our family and their children's children.

Proverbs 13:22 *"A good person leaves an inheritance for their children's children, but a sinner's wealth is stored up for the righteous. "*

The wife is there as a helpmate in all aspects, including the budget and finances. Doing what she can to help conserve, labor, and build an inheritance for her children. Being single, it is easy for us to spend money on frivolous things because no one other than us has to deal with the consequences. We pay our bills and then we decide where it goes and how much we want to go toward that new pair of shoes we saw on sale last week. We don't think much about being frugal because it's just us. When you are married, this mindset completely has to change. Everything you do and spend affects your husband and your family. You can't just go spend hundreds of dollars on shoes and purses! You have to sit with your partner and work out a plan for your finances. Are you ready for that? That means you can't just go all willy-nilly and shop all day without considering your partner. Now I know you're thinking, "What!? I have to sit and actually discuss with my partner where my money goes?" YES you do. Let me tell you why this is so important. When you get married, you are one with that man. Everything you do is done as a partnership, as a couple, as one unit. Out of respect for your partner, you should have agreements on these matters. Remember, what's mine is yours and what's yours is mine. It doesn't *just* say "What's yours is mine" does it? We fantasize and think a man will sweep us off of our feet and he will provide for us, make all the money, and we will just get up each day being loving and spending whatever we want with no thought behind it. Well, honey, let me break that fantasy for you now. This is a team effort. TEAM. Not saying that you won't ever be able to buy things that you desire, but I am saying that you have to consider each other and your family in those decisions. Are you ready to share the wealth? Are you ready to take on the responsibility of not just yourself but your husband and family? Do you budget your money well independently? If not, how can you expect to be able to budget with a spouse?

Proverbs 31:20-21 *"She opens her arms to the poor and extends her hands to the needy. When it snows, she has no fear for her household; for all of them are clothed in scarlet."*

God has called us all to go out into the world and to spread His word and also His love. Part of showing this love is giving help to the needy and taking care of the poor.

Deuteronomy 15:11 *"There will always be poor people in the land. Therefore I command you to be openhanded toward your brothers and toward the poor and needy in your land."*

As a wife, and as a family, it is good to never forget the needy and to actively seek out ways to provide for them. This is showing also the importance of having compassion and love towards others. It is a good example to her husband and also her family. The next passage is another reference to the importance of preparation. She has prepared her household so well that when disasters arise she is not shaken at all. Not just because she has prepared, but because she also knows the God she serves. This type of faith is SO important to you, as a woman, and to your spouse. There will be times that your husband will need that support when his faith is shaken because of external or internal circumstances. Though he is the leader of the household, his partner is a leader in rearing of the family in Christ. By her planning and her faith, she is not in fear. They have everything they need for any situation that arises.

Proverbs 31:22–23 *"She makes coverings for her bed; she is clothed in fine linen and purple.*
Her husband is respected at the city gate, where he takes his seat among the elders of the land."

This woman is dressed well and with dignity. She carries herself with honor and acts as royalty. Purple has always been seen to signify royalty, and it is very befitting to show the finesse of this woman. She not only dresses well but she also carries herself in that way. In our time, many of us dress in fine clothes but we act like filthy rags. Have you ever seen a beautiful woman who dressed very well and looks put together and nice? Then she opens her mouth and everything you envisioned goes away. Some of us are like this. We put a lot of time into the way we look but as soon as we speak the truth comes out; the heart and true soul of the person.

Luke 6:45 *"The good man out of the good treasure of his heart brings forth what is good; and the evil man out of the evil treasure* *brings forth what is evil; for his mouth speaks from that which fills his heart."*

We see that this woman is not only dressed in fine linen but she acts like a fine, well respected woman. This is why her husband is respected as well. A wife is a reflection of the husband just as children are a reflection of their parents. As a wife, you have a different responsibility than when you were single. When you are single, you still represent your parents and upbringing, but mostly what people see will be reflected back on you as an individual. When you are married, what you do will make people question your spouse and his character. Think about it. Let's say you see a couple together and they walk in and sit at the dinner table to accompany you. As the dinner goes on throughout the evening you notice that the wife gossips a lot and seems to critique every person that walks into the room. As the evening progresses it gets worse and she outwardly critiques someone's attire and starts an altercation with them. Now while all of this is going on, whom do you think everyone is looking at? Who do you think is the most embarrassed in the room? The husband. Everyone looks to him as if he is responsible for her and, trust me, the husband is thinking the same. People would also question why he would be with someone like that and question his character. In saying that, do you feel the way you act now is a reflection of a virtuous woman? You are single, but you are a child of God. So everything you do is a reflection of your Father, God. Do you feel how you act now is a reflection of Christ? Everything we do is a reflection of our husband and our Father, God. Does your reflection bring them honor?

Proverbs 31: 24–25 *"She makes linen garments and sells them, and supplies the merchants with sashes. She is clothed with strength and dignity; she can laugh at the days to come.*

This is yet another reference to her wisdom in laboring for her family and also taking care of those outside of her own home. I love how they continue to describe her as a woman of strength and dignity. The world tends to portray a woman that takes care of her home as meek and quiet. As someone who is soft spoken and moves only to her husband's command. This is not the case. This woman has just as much strength as her husband, but understands the importance of letting the husband lead the home. Her strength comes from her faith in God. This is why she is able to laugh at the days to come. She understands and knows that the future days are glorious because she knows the God that she serves and is wise. She doesn't nag her husband or worry. She doesn't worry her children with complaints and fright. She is calm and resting in the peace of God. That is strength. She knows that she has done everything she can on her end and the rest is up to God. She and her husband are sustained not by their own strength but by God's. Is your faith this strong? Are you so confident in your God that you can be at peace and not be anxious for anything? How do you handle thinking of the future now? Many of us worry about the future and in turn we stress ourselves out, and our bodies, because we are depending on our works instead of God's faithfulness. Learn how to depend on God in your life now and stay calm, whatever comes your way. If you practice and learn how to trust God now; it will benefit you tremendously when you have a spouse and family. As a wife and mother, they will look to you for how to react when tragedy or harm comes their way. If you exude a calm spirit, a spirit that trusts, they will do the same. This will also help your husband because it will build his faith and remind him that you all serve an amazing God. That's the type of support a companion needs.

Proverbs 31: 26–28 *"She speaks with wisdom, and faithful instruction is on her tongue. She watches over the affairs of her household and does not eat the bread of idleness. Her children arise and call her blessed; her husband also, and he praises her"*

This woman's words are wisdom to anyone who hears. For her to be wise, she studies her Word and shares it with others. She not only has wisdom from the Word, but she knows how to incorporate into earthly wisdom. Think about how, in the previous passage, it discusses the way she handles business in her home and outside of her home. She knows how to tend to her family but also how to manage the work world. In a different translation, it states that her words are wise and that she gives instruction with kindness. This is such an important aspect of this verse. See many of us have wisdom, but we become arrogant. We give instruction or wisdom but we do it in a way that is belittling. This verse explains that her instruction is full of wisdom but it is still also kind. There is a way to lead and instruct without making the other feel minute. As she gives wisdom she also watches over her household. She pays attention to everything that is going on in her home. Her husband, her children, the physical aspect of the home—everything. This is very important for a wife. She needs to be aware of what is happening in her home so she can be in tune with her family. As she is doing this, she is not concerned with anyone else's role as a wife; nor is she comparing herself to them. That is a hard one for many. We often look at what other people have and wonder why we don't have it. Think about how many times you've seen people envy the next door neighbor's car or even their children. This woman doesn't do that. This is important as well because we will see these things and sometimes stress out our spouses, because we want to attain the same. This is something you truly have to get out of your system or it will make your spouse feel he isn't doing enough. Be content and happy with the spouse and family God has given you. Towards the end of this passage, it explains the way the husband and children see her. They call her blessed! They praise her! Not because she is perfect, for no woman can be perfect. But they praise her because she is a loving, honorable, wise woman. The ending of the passage sums it up very well!

Proverbs 31:29–31 *"Many women do noble things, but you surpass them all."*
"Charm is deceptive, and beauty is fleeting; but a woman who fears the Lord is to be praised.
"Honor her for all that her hands have done, and let her works bring her praise at the city gate."

They praise her because she is special! She has something that other women don't possess and she doesn't possess it because of her own works, but because of God's strength and grace. It isn't about how pretty you are. It isn't about how fashionable you are or how charming. It is about a woman who serves and loves God with all of her heart and does everything she can to be pleasing in His sight. She is honored not only by her family but also by God.

Now I know after looking at all of the descriptions you are probably thinking, "WOW, there is no way I can do all of that!" And you are absolutely right. YOU can't do all of that. It is by God's strength that you can do it. It's not about perfecting every characteristic that you see described here. That is not possible. It is about your heart and willingness to serve God and to serve your family as God intends for us to do!

I want you to truly look at this description of this woman. We get so wrapped up in wanting a spouse that we forget that we have to be ready for a spouse. We forget, or sometimes are just completely unaware of, what it takes to truly be a wife; to truly be a companion to someone. I am not giving you all these descriptions to scare you by any means. I just don't want you to go into something without understanding the responsibility behind it. It's not all about the kisses, the love, and the cuddling. This is a serious covenant with someone that is not seen lightly by God at all. Being single has its blessings and also being with a mate has its blessings; and they both have struggles of their own as well. As a helpmate, you truly have to look outside of yourself and consistently think of others. I want you to be prepared for that. I want you to truly look at this life as the scripture I described above. It is a blessing being single because your desire and love is completely devoted to God. When you are married, you still love God, but your desires are for your husband and family. I know so many women who have said you truly have to be persistent and intentional in the time you spend with God. You will get so wrapped up in your husband and family that it takes true effort to keep that same relationship with God as you had when you were single. So enjoy this time! It's you and God and no one else. No one to interrupt you in your prayers. No one to interrupt you in your sleep. Just you and the Big Guy! Embrace the life God has given you now. When the time is right your spouse will come. Are you ready for the challenge?

Proverbs 31 is a glimpse into how God hopes to see His daughters in the home. I firmly believe that everything in the Word is inspired by the spirit and it even says so in the Bible.

> **2 Timothy 3:16** *"All Scripture is God-breathed and is useful for teaching, rebuking, correcting, and training in righteousness, God."*

This verse has given us specific instructions as women for a reason, because he knows what will cause harmony in the home. Every creation He has made has a purpose and it works best when it is walking out in the way He designed it to be. This excerpt gives you an idea of what it takes to truly be a wife, but trust me this is not all.

When we are single, we see married couples all around us and we dream one day to have what they have. We see the families together at church and praising God together. We see the husband and wife going out on dates and celebrating anniversaries. We see the postings on Facebook of their first child and the sweet surprise gifts that their spouse sent them for the day. We see all of the fantasy in real time and we sit there, scrolling, thinking, "Man, I'll be so happy to have that one day." What you have to remember is that you are seeing the result of a lot of work and prayer that is being done behind the scenes. They aren't showing you the prayer and patience it took to get their husbands to buy them "just because" gifts. They aren't showing you the many counseling sessions they went through to learn how to communicate better with each other. They aren't showing you the late nights staying up with their children. They are showing you the happy times; of which there are many. But please understand that every perfect gift from God has its responsibilities as well. I don't want you going into any relationship thinking that it is going to be an easy ride. Love is amazing and can be such a precious gift, but it takes work on your part and most of all a change in you. You cannot be the same person you are single when you are with a spouse. All of your priorities and commitments change and you have to change with it. All of us have things we are dealing with, and things of our personality and character that need some fine tuning. When you are single this is the perfect time to do this pruning so you can be the wife God needs you to be for your mate, and most of all so you can be the woman of God He has called you to be.

Chapter 3

Purge

When I was single, I thought I was such an amazing woman. I was intelligent, carried myself well, was active in the church, and thought I was a gem. I felt that any man would be beyond lucky to be with a woman like me. I think many of us think this way. We get ourselves boosted up by our friends and colleagues all the time.

"Girl you have two degrees, you need to be with an educated man!"
"Girl, you are too good to be dealing with that!"
"Girl, you dress way too nice for him! You need to get you a man like this!"

How many of us have had our friends tell us this? We hear it so often that we truly think we are a dime a dozen and a man needs to step up to our level to be with us and deserve any of our time. But guess what, you have things that need to change. Yep, I said it! I want to be the first to tell you that before a man comes into your life and you miss a good relationship because you think you are the "bomb.com" and that he is the only one who needs to get his self together. We put ourselves on a pedestal and feel we can do and be everything we need. We become so independent that we become our own man. We provide for ourselves. We make all the business decisions. We do what we want, when we want it and how we want it! We are the king of our own castle. Well naturally being in this position you pick up character traits that go along with it. You become dominant, because you are in a relationship with yourself and make all the decisions. You are independent; therefore you find it hard to trust other people, let alone some man, to take care of decisions. You think you—and ONLY you—know what is best. You become selfish. Now, when I say this, I am not trying to be harsh; it is just natural. You only have to worry about your needs so it's natural for you to become self-centered. You are probably impatient. Since we've been alone, we've made moves at our own pace and we expect others around us to do the same. We don't have to work on patience with ourselves because we do everything on our time. There are many other traits we pick up while being single and I will go over them soon. But what I want you to realize is that you have to be a totally different person when you are single than when you are someone's spouse. Before you are able to truly be a helpmate, you will have to purge these habits you have picked up. Not only will you need to purge these habits you've picked up from being alone, but you also need to get rid of areas in your life that need to be corrected, healed, and restored; such as addictions, past hurts, insecurities, and whatever issues you have been struggling with.

Purging is when you remove impurities, traits, or habits that are not pleasing to God's sight. It is the same as pruning, but more intense because it involves ridding ourselves of sins we haven't dealt with. Now is the time to do it; not when you get in a relationship with a man. See, God has allowed us to have this time of singleness so he can work on us and have our complete attention. He wants that one-on-one time with you to prepare you for Him and your spouse, and trust me, He is doing the same with the man He has called you to be with. Why is this so important? Because you want to be able to focus on your marriage, not trying to repair yourself. Your time of singleness is for that. So how do you purge, and what exactly do you need to purge? Well, some of this I can answer for you, and for some, I cannot. I will guide you on how to purge and also what traits you need to let go of before your spouse arrives. But, there are going to be some things you will have to work on that you personally know you are dealing with. We all have our different battles and you will have to truly seek God and ask Him to show you your ways that need to change. A relationship is not the place to fix yourself. Do that while you are single with God.

Psalm 25: 4-5 *"Show me your ways, Lord, teach me your paths.*
⁵ Guide me in your truth and teach me, for you are God my Savior,

and my hope is in you all day long."

Job 6:24 *"Teach me, and I will be silent; make me understand how I have gone astray.*

Independence

Oh, don't we just love that word! Being independent was the thing to be in my day and it still seems to be the praised life of many single women! Ever since the days of women's liberation, we have held on tight to our ability to do things that men said we couldn't and even show them we can do it even better! We have prided ourselves on this trait and love to show the world, and men, that we don't "have" to have them. I will never forget the song by *Destiny's Child* called *"Independent Woman"*. It glorified this independent life. When writing this book I actually went back to listen to the lyrics, and I quickly realized this glorifies a life that is not conducive to a woman who one day wants to truly be a wife—well, a Godly wife. Don't get me wrong. I think it is great to be able to take care of yourself, but not to the point that when a man comes into your life that you constantly remind him that you don't need him. I promise you, if you aren't saying it you are showing him in your actions

I remember how popular *Independent Woman* was with so many women. Soon after, many others came out glorifying the life of singleness and independence. Well, let me tell you my single independent ladies, if you don't adjust this attitude you will stay exactly that, SINGLE and INDEPENDENT. Women have come to the point where we pride ourselves in being able to provide for ourselves and we even cut down any man around us that tries to take that burden off of us. It's as if we see them as a threat to our lives and—to be honest—many times, it is out of fear. Ladies, if you want to be a wife one day, you will need to rid yourself of this perception. Men like to feel needed. It is natural for them to want to feel like the protector, the provider. They truly want to feel like your knight in shining armor and rescue you from the world. But no longer are they finding the damsels in distress. No, they are finding the Queens at war with themselves. Understand, it is great to know who you are, most importantly who you are in Christ. Also, as I stated previously, you don't have to wait for a spouse to be able to walk out your will for your life. But do not get this life of singleness and authority mixed up with the notion that you don't need a man in your life. What I want you to see is that God has called you to a purpose and a plan, but part of that purpose as well is being a wife, if it is God's will. Remember in the Proverbs description, this woman wore many faces. She was caring, smart, a business woman, and many other things that made her like royalty. But a Queen still respects her King. A true Queen understands her power, but knows her place. She doesn't undermine her King and makes sure to show him respect and honor in her actions and words. My Queens, don't become the King of your own castle. If you truly desire to be a helpmate, learn to trust the man that God brings into your life and respect his authority. Learn how to depend on him and find a balance in the responsibilities of duties and decisions. He wants to feel like you need him. He wants to know that you trust his decision-making and, most of all, RESPECT his decision-making. Don't look at being dependent as a bad thing. Trust me, it is not. There is nothing like surrendering to a man that can be trusted. We have the perception that we are not free when we submit, but in actuality there is freedom in submission. You will be surprised how natural and a joy it is to let the man lead. To let the man protect. To let the man provide. You can relax for once and not feel like you only have only yourself to depend on. You can relax, and guess what? Be a woman.

Selfishness

Being single can truly be a joyous experience. You wake up when you want to. You spend your money the way you want to. If you don't want to clean your place, you don't have to. If you want to pig out on ice cream and pizza for dinner, you can. If you don't want to shave until next spring, you don't. In anything and everything you do, as long as you are okay with it, that's all that matters. Every decision is made solely by you and you don't have to consider anyone else. It's the life. If you don't realize that right now, please take it all in. It's pure freedom. A lot of things change when a man enters your life and you are considering two instead of one. Don't feel bad. This is normal for any woman to get consumed with herself when she is alone. There are positives to this, because you have the time to solely focus on yourself and the things you want to change as well. But sometimes this alone time can grow into bigger issues when a man comes into your life and you don't even realize it. Here are some things we may do unconsciously when a man enters our lives, which are rooted in being selfish. These can transcend not only to intimate relationships, but any relationship (family, friends, etc.).

- We don't want to adjust our schedule to accommodate others.
- We don't want to adjust our spending habits to take into consideration two instead of one.
- We get used to being alone, so we aren't as willing to put work into getting to know someone new.
- We become protective of our happiness and serenity; therefore we have low tolerance for any screw-ups from a male. Even simple, common mistakes.
- We tend to not care as much about our physicality because we are the only one's seeing our bodies.
- We are not open to criticism, even if it's constructive.
- We avoid relationships to defend our theory that we don't need a man.

These are just a few of the habits we pick up, but there are plenty more. As I said before, don't feel bad about it. It is very normal when you are by yourself. I just want you to be aware of these habits so you can be sure to take steps to work on them. Relationships are the ultimate way God can form us into an example of Christ, because marriage is a complete change to selflessness. Everything becomes "we" and the "I" has to leave. Of course, when children come into the picture, this extends even more. So how can you work on this now? Be conscious of the moments you feel yourself falling into the habits mentioned above and others you may be aware of. Try now to adjust yourself to others around you. One thing I truly suggest is to stay in the attitude of giving your time and resources to those around you. Find a local community project to help with regularly. See what help your church may need. Contact your family and see if they need help at their house or maybe babysit some family member's kids. Whatever you decide to do, just stay in the motion of helping others and being involved. That way when a man enters your life it is natural for you to adjust who you are and what you have for someone else.

The "Save Me" Mentality

While we are waiting for our spouse to come into our lives we tend to fantasize and dream about the details of this man, yet we aren't looking at ourselves and what we have to offer. Don't think that this man will come into your life and fix issues that you need to fix by yourself. Think about it. If you went into a store and a woman offers you a device that is equipped and capable of everything intended, ready for use! Or a device that needs some work and you have to do the fixing. Obviously you would take the device that is ready and doesn't need you to come fix it! Too often as women, we get into the idea that a man is going to come our way and take care of problems we have that we can fix ourselves.

The man God brings into your life is not there to save you, but to help complement you. None of us are perfect and we all have things we need to work on, even when our spouse comes. But the ones you can take control of now; do so. When you meet your spouse, would you rather he is whole or incomplete? You want a man who has his life together and is able to sustain himself with only the help of God. Don't you think this type of man is looking for the same thing? Now, as I stated before, I am not glorifying the life of being independent but more so glorifying the life of being whole with you and God and taking care of issues before he arrives.

I think sometimes we as women get sucked into the Boaz story and think a man will come sweep us off of our feet and take care of all of our problems. Now understand God does sometimes bless you through a person and assist you in your issues. But if you remember Ruth was in the field. IN the field. Not thinking about the field. Not sitting on the sideline of the field waiting for someone to bring it to her. Not prancing around, looking pretty, and hoping a man would notice her. No, she was IN the field. She wasn't sitting around waiting for someone to come feed her and her mother-in-law. She went out and picked the grain that was left in the field herself and solved her own problems, and then God came to assist. Go out and do what you can for yourself now, if it's God's will, he will send a man who will assist you, but not save you. Only God can save, not man.

I want you to do a little exercise. Below, write down the qualities you are looking for in a man. Afterwards, write down what type of woman would complement him. Are you this woman? If not, what can you do to get there? What things can you work on?

Your Ideal Mate   Your Ideal Mate Match

_____   _____

_____   _____

_____   _____

_____   _____

_____   _____

_____   _____

_____   _____

_____   _____

_____   _____

_____   _____

_____   _____

_____   _____

_____   _____

Here are some tips to help you transition from the single life to a relationship and some do's and don'ts of when your spouse finds you.

From Single to Wife to Be

1. Start seeking wise counsel for your finances and life decisions. This will get you used to having someone else look at your life and give you a perspective from the outside. This will also help you get out of the "sole control" mindset.

2. Sit down and write out all of the things you spend your money on each month. Now imagine having a spouse or child. Your husband has asked you to pull back on some of your expenses. What things could you live without?

3. Start spending time in the company of Godly women who are married. See how they treat their husbands. Ask them how they transitioned from being single into a wife and mother.

4. Study the Bible on being a wife and also marriage. This will help you see the true expectations of a wife and the seriousness of the covenant you make with God and your husband.

5. Speak with women who have been married, whether divorced or widowed. Preferably someone who is not bitter and has been down the path of forgiveness. It is AMAZING when you can hear the wisdom of these women. Let them teach you some things that maybe they would have done differently. They will truly help you look at relationships differently and let go of the small things that don't matter.

6. Offer to babysit someone's children if you want to be a mother one day. Not only will this help you see the interaction between you and the kids but it will also be an act of kindness to help you learn to live selfless.

7. Develop a close and intimate relationship with God. When you learn to love God and be obedient to Him, you will have no problem loving your husband and being submissive to him.

8. Just as in *Proverbs 31*, learn to take care of every aspect of the home.

9. Learn to be complete by yourself. Don't get this confused with independence. When I say complete, I want you to learn to go to God for the needs you have and let Him fill voids instead of expecting a man to do so. This will truly help you with being disappointed when you don't get everything from your spouse as you expected. This is unrealistic. Only God can be your everything.

10. Work on truly having a gentle and quiet spirit. Many women confuse this with being a mute, but this is not what this entails. A gentle and

quiet spirit is a woman who can have peace regardless of what situation she is in. She is able to be patient and trust God and the husband that is leading her without causing more tension or confusion. Learn how to attain peace regardless of what is going on around you. To be the gentle, calm spirit that brings peace to any situation.

Do's and Don'ts

1. Do not pursue the man or the relationship. Let him lead you in the relationship. If you start pursuing and leading now, you will ALWAYS do so.
2. Do not belittle him. Yes, you may have more degrees than he does. Yes you may even know more than he does. But is it worth hurting his pride? No.
3. Do not embarrass him in public. Many women tend to correct their spouses or argue with them in front of others, and this can hurt a man's pride tremendously. Even if he is wrong about something, wait until you are in private and bring it up.
4. Do not talk to him like a child. You are not his mother, you are his wife.
5. Do not bring up past issues or forgiven actions. You said you forgave him, so don't bring it up. This happens A LOT in relationships and can slowly tear it down.
6. Don't push him to change. That is God's job. As a wife, bring up your concerns and then pray and leave the rest up to God.
7. Do let him be a gentleman. Too often men try to open doors for us, or carry our things and we say, "Oh, I got it." Don't do that. Let him be a man.
8. Do give him time to do what you've asked of him. Nagging doesn't make him move faster.
9. Do show him respect in your speech and actions. Numerous men bring up in counseling that they don't feel their spouse respects them.
10. Do be loving, supportive, encouraging, and his best friend. Men truly just want support and want to feel their mate has their back.

Chapter 4

The Perception of Boaz

A ll our lives we've heard the phrase of finding "The One." This guy sounds so perfect and gives you the idea that there is a guy out there who was made just for you and is going to be everything you ever dreamed and imagined; that when you meet this guy, your eyes will meet and you'll know: he's the exact guy you've been waiting for all this time. We see it all the time. Disney movies, romantic comedies, and even hear friends tell us that when they met their match, it was love at first sight. That they knew immediately when they met them that they were going to spend the rest of their lives with them. I think we all are waiting for this guy. We go from one failed relationship to the next and we have set in our minds that he just wasn't the one and one day everything will work out. Now I do believe that there is a man out there that God knows is the best man for you. He is a man that loves Him and will know how to treat, respect, and cherish you just as God does. The issue comes in when we think that this man will be perfect. That we won't have problems with him as we did our past guys and we will run in the meadows, holding hands, and off into the rainbows. Well, I am here to tell you now, yes, he will be better than your past but He will be far from perfect and you will be far from perfect as well.

Marriage is a beautiful thing, but many of us go into it expecting this man to swoop into our lives like Superman and save us from all our distresses, heartaches and pains. That he will make all things perfect and our lives will change forever. Many of us get this concept from the all-so-popular story of Ruth and Boaz. This story has been used numerous times by women when speaking of their long-awaited future mate. Whether claiming they want to always be ready for their Boaz, or stating they are waiting for their Boaz, this name has been used as a visual concept of the man we've been waiting for God to bring into our lives. The funny thing is that no one ever thinks to themselves about Ruth. We glorify Boaz so much that we forget that Ruth had to be some type of woman for a man such as Boaz to come into her life. While you are waiting for your Boaz, or even feel you have found your Boaz, ask yourself, "Am I a Ruth?" There are many misconceptions of this story and I want to point out the misconceptions of Boaz and also point out some important characteristics of Ruth. God will bring a good man into your life, but please don't have a particular concept of him in your mind, because you will then put this pressure on him to be this man and drive him away. Remember that your husband may be heaven sent, but he is still just a man. He is not God, but a man. Before a man enters your life, realize he is only a man and will not encompass everything you need as if he is God.

He Is Not Your Savior

Many of us are in different situations in our lives and are in dire need of help and assistance. Whether you are a single mom, divorced, or maybe just never had a father figure in your life, we all have needs and hope that a man entering our lives will change the situation. Some of us are dealing with debt we've incurred from school or maybe just our personal habits. Some of us have been left with baggage from past husbands or mates who aren't helping in areas they promised. Some of us have children with no help from the father and need assistance. The list can go on and on. We wait and we wait, hoping that one day our Boaz will find us and fix all of these issues. Well guess what, loves: that's A LOT of pressure to put on a man.

Many women read the story of Ruth and Boaz and see that Ruth was very poor and came from a family that had nothing. She took a risk and stayed with her mother-in-law and had to fend for herself and her. She had nothing and was so desperate that she had to pick left over grains from herders. Now in the process of her doing this, Boaz sees her and eventually, one day decides he wants to marry her, and her and her mother-in-law's lives change forever. Many women focus on this one moment and think the same will happen to them.

But Boaz didn't save Ruth, God did. God was the one to orchestrate this entire ordeal and honored Ruth's faithfulness and obedience. Boaz was merely a vessel God used to bless Ruth. But we do not honor Boaz, we honor God. Don't become so concerned about your appearance in public because you may meet your Boaz, when you should be focusing on God and worrying about your spiritual appearance to Him. Don't constantly wait for a man to save you that you focus on him as a savior and forget that God is your savior. He can use any person or thing on this earth to save you in your circumstances. That saving may come through a man, or it may come through Him simply blessing you with what you need. Stop looking around for a man and look up.

He Is Not Superman

Getting into a marriage it is a great thing to k now you have a man to depend on, especially if he has a true relationship with God and accountability towards Him. He is there to provide, protect and cover the household. We look to him to take care of us and the family and put our trust in him. Sometimes as the role men play in our lives we do have to remember that he can only do so much on his own and that he truly has to depend on God. Though it is his place to be in this role you can't expect him to be able to fix and do everything. Some things will be out of his control and he can only do what he can. God on the other hand is limitless. He can do and be anything and can truly take care of it all. Always remember that. Your husband, or awaited Boaz is not Superman. He will not be able to provide some things sometimes. He will not be able to fix every appliance that breaks in the home. He will not be able to solve every problem that arises as a family. Will he try? Yes. Will he fail sometimes? Yes. Will he tell you he can't do some of the things you ask? Sometimes, no.

It is in a man's pride to want to be able to do all these things but realistically sometimes they can't. When this occurs remember that God is the one that has everything we need and ask Him to help your husband and to also help you be patient and trust things will work out. This will help you from becoming angry or impatient with your mate when things don't work out as planned. When issues come up such as him losing a job, or something as simple as a bill getting paid, instead of becoming angry, stop and remember who the source of everything you have and need is. You will soon learn to relax and be anxious for nothing but through prayer and supplication make your requests known to God. You will remember that things will work out, because you are not dependent on man but God.

He is Not a "Yes" Man

I think many of us think that when a man comes, we will be able to ask for anything and everything and if he loves us, he will provide it. We somewhat turn into the mindset of a daddy's girl and beg and plead for us to get our way. Now if this man is mature and has a sound mind, loves God, and truly cares about the state of the home and you, there will not always be a "yes" for everything, just like with God's answer isn't a "yes" for everything. God always says he will provide our needs and he even brings up that He will provide the desires of our hearts. But some take this idea of desires and infer that this means our wants. I want you to take a look at this scripture;

> **Psalm 37:3–5,** *"Trust in the LORD, and do good; so shalt thou dwell in the land, and verily thou shalt be fed. Delight thyself also in the LORD: and he shall give thee the desires of thine heart. Commit thy way unto the LORD; trust also in him; and he shall bring it to pass."*

Now many people focus on the part where God explains He will give you the desires of your heart. But notice before that it says that you will trust in Him with all your heart and delight in His ways. Now when delighting yourself with someone, you take time to commune with them. It is a joy to be with them. You delight in His word, promises, and who God is in your life. Beyond that, you commit your ways to Him and trust Him. See, when you do all of that, your desires will change from your own to the desires that God has. You will find yourself not wanting things of this world but wanting the things God desires for your life. You also trust God and know that He will bring to pass what is best for you.

Well, you have to be the same way with your potential mate and husband. He isn't just someone who is going to give and give what you want just because you ask. Now he will sometimes give you things just to bring your joy. The Word even says that if we, as evil doers, are givers of good things, why would God not be a giver of good things as well? But at the same time He uses sound wisdom and does what is best for us eternally instead of presently. Think the same of your mate and give him that same respect. Also realize you can get some things for yourself. God has given us wisdom and the ability to attain some things on our own. Remember in the previous chapters when we looked at the woman of *Proverbs 31*, she was a woman of many trades! She didn't just sit and wait for her husband to do everything, she had some worth and wit to herself as well. Trust your husband. Remember you are a virtuous woman, not a spoiled princess.

He Is Not Your Sole Provider

Philippians 4:19 *"But my God shall supply all your need according to his riches in glory by Christ Jesus."*

Understand that you potential mate is only a vessel. Everything he has and does is because of God's anointing and gifts and he can only do it through God's power. God reminds us in His Word multiple times that He will provide everything that we need; everything. Many times we disregard the fact that it says, "...all your needs," but not necessarily all of our wants. Your husband's responsibility is to supply your needs and as he chooses he can supply some of your desires and wants. Out of love many of us do this, and I am sure your future mate will do the same. But let's say your husband only supplies the needs of the family and home, will you be satisfied? Will you complain because he isn't giving you what you want as well? I hope not. Not because you are being mute and not expressing your need to feel loved through gift giving, but because you are respecting his effort and willingness to take care of the family. Your husband is not the only person that can supply you with some of your desires and wants, God can.

Matthew 7:11 *"If you, then, though you are evil, know how to give good gifts to your children, how much more will your Father in heaven give good gifts to those who ask him?"*

Whether it comes to the personal desires you have for yourself, or maybe some desires you have for the family or household, realize that God is a giver of good things as well. If you truly desire to have gifts given to you because it makes you feel loved, then be sure to express that to him but not in a way that makes him feel he is not doing enough. When we as women pull and pull on our men for so many things, it makes them feel they are not adequate enough to take care of us nor make us happy. Be grateful for what he does provide and ensure he knows that. When he sees how happy this makes you, he will want to do even more just to put a smile on your face. But whatever things are not being done, pray about these things and trust that if it is something that will not deter you or your family away from God, He will provide it.

He Will Be Looking for Ruth

Throughout the story of Ruth and Boaz, Ruth decided to take a chance with her mother-in-law, Naomi, and this was not an easy decision. She knew by staying with her, she risked the possibility of not being cared for by a man and Naomi and she being forced to fend for themselves. Regardless of the risks, she decided to stay loyal and God blessed her for this decision. Now Ruth could have easily kept to herself and stayed in a "woe is me" attitude, and waited for God to bring a man in her life to fix their problems. But she didn't leave as Orpah did; she stayed and decided to trust God. But while she waited, Ruth did everything she could on her end to help her situation. Even though they could not do much, she got up every day and picked food from left over grains from herders each day. She was in the field putting her own works and faith into practice and trusted God each day to provide. As she consistently did this, one day Boaz notices her and informs his workers to leave more grain each day. Without her knowing, Boaz shows her favor. One of the reasons Boaz does this is that he heard of her story.

Ruth 2:10–11 *¹⁰ At this, she bowed down with her face to the ground. She asked him, "Why have I found such favor in your eyes that you notice me—a foreigner?"*

¹¹ Boaz replied, "I've been told all about what you have done for your mother-in-law since the death of your husband—how you left your father and mother and your homeland and came to live with a people you did not know before. ¹² May the LORD repay you for what you have done. May you be richly rewarded by the LORD, the God of Israel, under whose wings you have come to take refuge."

Before he even meets Ruth, Boaz hears good things about Ruth and is intrigued. What will a man hear about you when he asks about you? Will they be good things? Things of honor? Things that will make him want to meet you? Keep this in mind as you wait for your prince. Boaz notices her tenacity, love for her family and her strong spirit. He was attracted to this quality and wanted to take her in as his own. He saw her as a great complement to him and his heritage and wanted this woman to be a part of his life. The key to this story is that Ruth took action for herself. She didn't wait to be saved, she did what she could and she was noticed. How do you expect for your Boaz to find and notice you when you are never in the fields? Wherever you are, whoever you are, you still need to continue on with your life and be the woman that a man like Boaz was looking for. He wasn't looking for a woman who was depressed, sad, and helpless. But a woman who took her situation and did what she could on her part! Get in the fields, or your harvest will never take root!

Being found by the conceptual idea of a man like Boaz is on the mind of many Christian women. We all are waiting for our King to arrive but we aren't preparing ourselves to be Queens. Ensure that you are a woman that a man wants to be found by and also equipped to be his complement. Whether single or engaged be aware of what the husband's role truly is and not put so much responsibility on him as if He is God. God is still your provider, savior, redeemer and first love. Prepare yourself for this role now and take away the misconceived idea of Boaz saving you from all your sorrows and cares. God said to cast your cares upon HIM and He will sustain you, not your husband. Make sure to read this story of faithfulness, trust and loyalty towards God and family. It is an amazing testimony when we step out on faith and trust God to supply our needs and put aside our need to be comfortable. He will notice your sacrifice and honor you.

Chapter 5

Unconditional Love

Marriage is the perfect way for God to mold us to be more like Christ. Why do I say this? Because God's love is unconditional. During your vows, this word will come up and sometimes people don't truly understand the full context of unconditional love. Unconditional love means loving someone regardless of the circumstance. This is beyond being sick or broke, but even when that person treats you like nothing. When they don't do what they promised. When they don't do their part as a husband. When they forget your birthday and anniversary. Regardless of how THEY are acting, you still love. Jesus died on the cross for us while we were still sinning. He didn't say, "Oh, when they stop lying, I'll get on the cross for them," or, "Oh, when they stop beating me, then I'll die on the cross for them." No, he got on the cross *despite* how we were acting, because he loved us.

Romans 5:8 *"But God demonstrates his own love for us in this: While we were still sinners, Christ died for us"*

That's love. When we marry, sometimes we don't realize how serious unconditional love has to be portrayed and even how hard it can be when you aren't receiving love back from your spouse. You love and respect them not based on what they are doing, but based on your obedience to Christ. You have a responsibility as a wife to uphold your vows regardless of what has changed in him or the marriage. This applies to your husband as well. This is pleasing to God's sight, and expected as a spouse. When I was married, this became extremely difficult for me when we were going through hard times. I loved him dearly, but when things didn't go the way I expected, showing love to him became harder and harder by the day. But I had to do it. Not for him, but for God. I still made his lunch. I still cleaned. I was still there intimately despite how I felt. It was my duty as his wife and an expression of unconditional love. Also, showing love to him, despite his actions, will turn his ways around. No, not your nagging, but your love towards him.

Grasping the art and understanding of unconditional love is vital before you get into any marriage. I truly believe that many divorces occur simply because they do not understand the art of unconditional love. Many of them have ended stating they fell out of love with the spouse, or because the spouse changed. But if you truly love the person you married, none of that will happen, nor will it matter. You love him in all the changes. You make a vow between him and God and nothing breaks it. Go into your marriage having set in your mind that, regardless of what happens, you will stick by your spouse's side. All marriages go through hard times, but, sadly, many have divorced their spouse right in the midst of this struggle. But every rough patch soon heals and comes out for the better. You have to stick by your spouse through everything. If you have set in your mind that you will work out anything and everything. That you will be patient with your spouse. Love your spouse regardless of the circumstances. You will be able to be a wife that bears all for him. Now please do not mistake this with physical abuse being acceptable. That is not of God's character. I wouldn't resort to divorce automatically. If things like this come up then separate yourselves, pray, let him seek counseling, and leave the rest up to God.

I truly want women to be prepared for the reality of marriage. Too often we get into marriages and love being involved as long as it's rosy and peachy all the time. But this will not always be the case. I truly suggest that you talk to other couples. Many couples that you see that love each other unconditionally and seem to be the perfect couple have been through some rough patches, but they endured. Talk to women on how they stayed by their spouse through it all. Learn from their experiences. Ask them what helped them stick by their husband despite the hard times. Surround yourself with what you want to become as a wife, and couples that display what you desire for your own marriage.

A good way to truly understand this concept is learning to love your enemies as God has instructed. This is a great example of loving someone despite how they are treating you.

Matthew 5:44 *"But I tell you, love your enemies and pray for those who persecute you."*

Luke 6:35 *But love your enemies, do good to them, and lend to them without expecting to get anything back. Then your reward will be great, and you will be children of the Most High, because he is kind to the ungrateful and wicked.*

Loving those who have done us wrong can be so hard. Especially when they are people from whom you didn't expect it; such as your friends or family members. But we all know that it definitely happens. It's hard because in the world today they teach you that you love those who love you and hate those that hate you. It's innate for us to victimize ourselves and feel completely justified to hate the person because they were wrong. As the world has put it, "Eye for an Eye and Tooth for a Tooth." But this isn't God's way at all. He expects us to love them, treat them well, and even bless them, regardless of what they have done to us. This not only shows them the love of God, but it frees you from un-forgiveness. We hold grudges toward other people as if we are getting them back for their wrongs, when in actuality we are just hurting ourselves. When you show love to them, it blesses you and helps you to heal from their wrongs. God will take care of them. You just be obedient and love them as obedience to Christ.

Proverbs 25: 21-22 *"If your enemy is hungry, give him food to eat; if he is thirsty, give him water to drink.*
In doing this, you will heap burning coals on his head, and the Lord will reward you."

When you learn to love those who have done you wrong in the past, or those who are even doing you wrong presently, it will be much easier to do so with your spouse. Imagine having to love someone in your own home that is treating you like an enemy. Understand that this happens sometimes. But if he truly loves you—if he truly wants to spend the rest of his life with you—his heart will change, but let God change him. To many times we try to change people and no one has the power to do that but God. Praying for your spouse is one of the toughest weapons you can use to help your spouse and marriage. What is so amazing about this prayer time about your spouse, you will find God changing you in the process as well. A book I suggest getting is *The Power of a Praying Woman* by Stormie Omartian. This will be a great book to add to your journey of becoming a wife and when you are married. It truly shows the importance of giving your concerns over to God and trusting Him with the process instead of yourself. I used this myself when I had issues within my marriage. Though God's will was done, it helped change my thinking on my husband and also showed me my faults. What's amazing is that, during your prayer time while you are asking God to work on issues within your husband, God will change you in the process as well. I truly believe if I had known about this book before, I would have handled a lot of our issues differently than I did.

You have to take hold the gift of unconditional love to have any relationship be successful. He will disappoint you, and you will disappoint him. He won't be everything you imagined; and guess what: you won't either. Sometimes we put such high standards on other people, yet we would hate it if someone did us the same way. Love isn't about getting everything you want. Love isn't about being happy all the time. Love is about expressing compassion and sacrifice towards one another as Christ does for us. If you keep in mind all God has done for us, despite all we have done, you will give more grace to those around you as well.

He Is Not Your Fulfillment

It is hard for us to accept the true understanding of unconditional love, because we have placed in our minds that the spouse we are with is here to make us happy and give us a fulfilling life. That is not what marriage is about. Many women go into their relationships thinking that their awaited joy will come from a man, and they are quickly disappointed when they realize this is far from the truth. Unconditional love starts with your understanding that he will not be able to fill every void, insecurity, and lack of fulfillment you have in your life. That is not his job and it never will be. Anytime you look to other people to fulfill a need that you have, you are bound to be disappointed. Every void that you have in your life needs to be dealt with internally and, most of all, with God. When we are lacking in certain areas of our lives we tend to pressure a man to compensate for the void. Sometimes, this can be the reason men feel they are not enough of a man for you and fear commitment. You cannot be that dependent on any man or external object to make you feel a certain way. You have to deal with your issues and conquer them head on with Christ.

What, in your present life, are you not satisfied with? Is it your body? Is it a lack of fulfillment at work? Go through this list and check the statement that you identify with the most. This will help you see where you are lacking a sense of confidence, joy, or fulfillment.

I frequently think of how I need to lose/gain weight. _____

I tend to switch jobs frequently. _____

I look to guys to make me feel attractive. _____

When I am not dating anyone, I assume it is because
of my looks. _____

Previous guys I've dated have expressed I am too needy. _____

I am always changing my look to fit the present trend. _____

I don't like to go out unless I look perfect. _____

I feel I still need to find myself. _____

I question if I made the right career choice. _____

I didn't have a father nor father figure in my life. _____

I feel odd when I don't have at least one guy friend in
my life. _____

I have stayed in a relationship with a guy, even after I
found him unfaithful or dishonest. _____

I generally find myself bringing up the idea of a
relationship to who I'm dating _____

I envy those who are in a relationship. _____

I think something is wrong with me because I do not
have a boyfriend. _____

I tend to go back to my exes. _____

Though there are multiple questions I could ask you, I just wanted to give you an idea of your present mindset. Sometimes we don't realize how we think of ourselves until we sit down and see it on paper. Look at some of the responses with which you identified yourself. Sit down and understand what led you to allow certain people or behaviors into your life. Why do you think this way about yourself? Why did you take the actions you did? Beyond these, you know what parts of your life you want to change and also what you feel is missing. Or possibly you need to fill a void in your life, but you are unsure of what is missing. Whatever it may be, this needs to be found before a man comes into your life. I don't want you to get into a relationship, get distracted, and then when the high of the relationship is over, the void will reveal its ugly head. This is the best time for you to fill those voids. So I'm sure you are wondering how to do this and even where to start. How can you find your fulfillment? How can you have joy now? How can you fill the voids?

Matthew 6:33 *"But seek ye first the kingdom of God, and his righteousness; and all these things shall be added unto you."*

Seek Your Maker

As a teenager I can remember thinking I knew who I was, what I wanted, and who I was going to be. No one could tell me differently, and if you tried, I would completely ignore your opinion. Many of us have thought we knew what we wanted to do in our careers. We thought we knew what type of man we wanted and also the type of lifestyle we wanted to live. When you think about the decisions you have made, based on who you thought you were, have you always been accurate? Probably not. Honestly, we don't truly know what will bring us joy; only God does. I made so many career moves in my life because I was sure the "next" job would be the one. I soon realized the jobs weren't the issue, I was. For you to know what will bring you fulfillment in life, you need to seek God and ask Him to show you. God allows us to make our own plans and maneuver our lives, because He knows that, if He just told us what to do, we would be rebellious and feel we didn't have a choice in our lives. He allows this because He wants us to see that He is the one that knows best, not us. When I finally realized that I didn't know what's best, I surrendered my plans to God and that's when things became clear. Instead of moving from place to place or from one hobby to the next, just be still. Ask God to show you His plan for your life and what He has called you to do. Your fulfillment will come when you find your purpose.

Confront Your Insecurities

From reality TV, movies, music videos, and celebrities it is so easy for us to become insecure about our bodies and also our lifestyle. From the implants to the permanent make up it seems we have to be perfect to compare to the physical beauty all around us.

I still remember the commercial from Dove that exposed how much digital editing is done to models to exude the beauty of perfection. I was so glad Dove showed this to the world because so many women are trying to compare themselves to other women and change themselves to look like the deception of a real woman. It is easy for us to feel we are not enough, but you need to realize that you are. Whether you are insecure about your body, looks, or current lifestyle, you have to remember that you are only seeing what the people want you to see. No one can make you feel comfortable and confident in who you are and what you have but yourself. You have to decide what you are happy with and make changes where you feel it is needed. But do not make these changes to look like someone else. Make changes to look like the best you that you have in mind.

Remember that it is not your physical appearance that should get all of your attention, but your character. Ask God to help you feel confident and secure in who He has made you. I remember realizing one day that my insecurity about how I look is basically telling God that I don't like His design. You are who you are for a reason. Accept who you are. When you accept the person God has made you, no man can break the way you feel about yourself physically because you are not dependent on him to validate you. God has validated you. That is all you need. Whoever you are, and whatever you have, that is enough for you and nobody can question that.

Depend on God, Not Man

When we have issues arise in our lives—or just had a bad day—we all have that one person we feel we can call to make us feel better. It could be your best friend, parents, or boyfriend; someone that you know you can depend on any time of the day and night. Every time we call or meet up with them, they lift our spirits and we thank God that they are in our lives. I mean, what would we do without them? I will tell you what you would do without them, live. God loves for us to have companionship and Godly counsel. He states this in His word. But too often we become extremely dependent on others and we ignore God. How would your life look if you went to God first with your problems? How would your life change if every time you were having a bad day, you prayed first? God wants to be your first responder to every situation. He is always right there with you, why aren't you going to Him for help? I think many of us do this because we forget God is there. Why do we forget? Because we spend more time in the world, rather *than* in the Word. We forsake our communion with God for TV, social media sites, food, and among other earthly indulgences. All of these things are completely fine, but when they are done in the correct order and moderation. I have seen God strip others, and even myself, of the things I am most dependent on and have put before Him. He does this to remind us that He should be first before anything and anyone.

Matthew 6:24 *"No one can serve two masters, for either he will hate the one and love the other, or he will be devoted to the one and despise the other. You cannot serve God and money."*

Know Yourself and Balance Your Needs

As women, we have many needs, especially emotional needs. We want to feel loved, accepted, needed, cared for, protected, approved, and the list can go on and on. Each day we can go from one mood to the next and we expect for anyone around us to adjust to those moods. When others around us don't adjust to our needs, we reach out to the things outside of people to fulfill them. We grab our ice cream, go shopping and max out our credit cards, play on Facebook, or anything that will fill that empty void. Learn how to deal with these emotions and needs in a healthy way now so you will not strain your spouse or family. This will take a lot of pressure off of your spouse. Men have a lot on their plate with being the head of the family, protector, and provider. Though you are there for each other and your family, some things can be handled on your own and most of all, you can go to God. Being single, you already know what your needs and moods are and when you find yourself becoming a little bit needier than usual. We all do it. While you are single, find ways that will make it easier for those around you during those times. Whether you go to the gym to calm your nerves or have a girls night out, find out how to take care of yourself in the areas where you can. This will help keep the peace between you and your spouse and the peace in your entire home. I am sure you have heard the phrase "A happy wife means a happy life." I truly believe it when people say that when a woman is upset, irritable, or just plain frustrated, the entire house suffers. Sometimes we as women truly don't realize how much influence we have in the home.

Proverbs 25:24 *"It's better to live alone in the corner of an attic than with a quarrelsome wife in a lovely home."*

Don't be this woman. We all go through our moods, and may not get our way sometimes, but be the woman in *Proverbs 31*. Where the father and children praise her, a woman that brings peace into the home, not emotions that are in disarray and places her needs before her family. Will you get frustrated sometimes? Yes. Will your husband or family hurt your feelings sometimes? Yes. Will you become so frustrated that you just need to leave the house to regroup? Yes. The issue isn't the way you are feeling. The issue is how you deal with it. Learn to handle your feelings and emotions now, so when you are living with someone, it will not cause a strain on them. The only one that knows you better than yourself is God. Other than God, only you know who you are and what calms you and also what gets you riled up. Get yourself in check before there are others around that it will affect as well. You will be surprised how things such as this, if not handled properly, can make a man never want to be home. He will leave work and go out with the boys or just anywhere that can keep him away from more stress. Make it your goal to be a place of peace for your spouse. A place where he can relax, calm his nerves and not feel pressured as he does in the real world.

Chapter 6

Only God Can Change Man

Tatiana: "Girl, I met this guy last night and he is so cute! We are going out on a date next week."

Layla: "Really, where did you meet him?"

Tatiana: "I met him at the grocery store. He was with his little girl and they were grocery shopping for dinner."

Layla: "Aww. How sweet!"

Tatiana: "Yeah, girl, only thing is he just got out of a marriage and still going through the divorce. He comes off a bit possessive, but I like the attention. He doesn't really know Christ, but we are going to start going to church with each other."

Layla: "Wow, girl he sounds like he has a lot going on. You think it's a good idea to date him? I thought you wanted a guy who loved God this time and knew what he wanted?"

Tatiana: "Oh girl, I can deal with that. He is going to start going to church with me."

Layla: "What about the marriage though? You sure you want to date someone that is still married?"

Tatiana: "I mean technically they aren't together anymore. He is just going through a hard time. He doesn't really like to talk about it too much, but I know he doesn't want her anymore."

Layla: "Okay, Tatiana. I can't control you but that doesn't sound like a good situation and I don't want you to be disappointed."

Tatiana: "Girl, I will be fine. I can tell he is really into me. People change and maybe, since he will be around me, it will help him get to know Christ. I'll tell you how the date goes! I'm so excited!"

How many of us have been Tatiana, or been the friend listening to what we know will end in a disaster? We all have been here before and completely blind to what we know is the truth. As single women, we do this quite often solely out of desperation and sometimes naiveté. We want attention and someone to love, and love us, so bad that we will take anyone and completely ignore the red flags. We go into the relationship or dating scene and we ignore the flags over and over again. The constant cancellation of dates. The calls that only come at night and never during the day. The empty promises that they make. We see all the flags but we ignore them and when the relationship ends in heartache and pain we act surprised. Then we ask ourselves, "How did I not see this?" when the signs were there all along. We go into dating, relationships, and, many times, even marriage seeing signs of who a person is and we ignore them or think we can change them. This is the wrong way of thinking. I had to learn it the hard way, but you have to accept people for who they are. If they don't have what you need, that's okay. Go your separate ways and find your match.

As women, we love to nurture and take on projects. We love to fix things and take those under our wings and help mold them into something better. The issue with this nurturing side is that we try to do the same thing to men we meet. We see an issue that we know isn't best for us and we either ignore it out of desperation or prepare ourselves to take on a project of changing the man. Wrong thinking. There is a difference between molding a man and changing a man. When molding a man, he is already in that state of being but just needs some minor tweaking. Changing someone involves you completely molding them into a different person and being.

Whether getting married or dating, understand that you need to accept a man for who he is and, most of all, believe exactly what you are seeing in the fruits he is bearing; not what he is saying. In every relationship, there are adjustments that will be made, that's normal. You are bringing two people together who are trying to become one and that can be a tough mold to make, but possible. But there is a difference between adjusting as a couple and changing a person from who they really are.

When we meet a guy, we look at the way he dresses, how he talks, how he spends money, who his friends are, and more. We pick out immediately what needs to change and calculate in our minds what we can tweak to fit what we "really" want in a man. Sadly, sometimes we become so desperate in wanting a man that we take what we can get and calculate what we can do to form him into what we truly want. We do this and truly feel it is of no harm. But it is not only of harm to him but also to ourselves. There are so many dangers that come with wanting to change a man and not accepting him for who he truly is. This is very important to take notice of *before* you walk down an aisle with your soon-to-be husband or simply decide to get into a relationship with someone. Realize that exactly who you are seeing right now is exactly who he is and you cannot change it.

So what's so harmful about overlooking the big red flags we see in a man when we meet him or get to know him? What's the harm of taking on the project of trying to mold a man into what we want? Also, what are the dangers of not accepting a man for who he is, and trying to force our perceptions of what we think he should be? Let's take a moment and see.

Rebellion

Every time I would meet a guy, I would size up who he was and immediately critique him. I would compare him to the type of guy I had in my mind and figure out a plan on how can I get him to look and be this way. I think we all do this; but unconsciously. We take the things they have that we do like and think we can change the things we don't like or we can convince them that it needs to change. We think it is harmless to feel this way but it is not fair to him, or to yourself. The danger of doing this is that some guys will adjust themselves solely to be with you, but not for the betterment of themselves. Trust me; I've seen it for myself in relationships. When we as women see this, we think that it is sweet and feel that this guy really loves us and wants to change all of these things

57

for us. But here is the problem; it won't last for long. When you are trying to change someone, especially if he is doing it only for you, he will eventually resort back to who he TRULY is. Why? Because you changed him on the outside, but nothing changed on the inside. He will play the role as long as he can, but after only so long, his real self will begin to seep out. See what you have to realize is that for you to truly change someone they have to see the intent behind the change and the value in the change.

For instance, let's say that the man you are dating likes to spend money on frivolous things and you value saving money to be resourceful and also to plan for the future. He really wants to be with you and you nag him about this constantly. Ultimately, he gets tired of hearing you talk about it so he begins to watch the way he spends and actually starts to take part of his check and save it. But he is doing it solely to keep you off of his back. Eventually, you calm down and you stop keeping tabs on him and his savings. Next thing you know he comes home with a brand new motorcycle and you are furious. You thought he changed right? What would make him go buy this motorcycle? Because he was doing it to keep you quiet, not because his morals nor values had changed. Whether you stop paying attention to his habits, or because he becomes angry with you and could care less about your feelings anymore, the true person that he wants to be will come out. If a man is changing his ways make sure it's because he sees the true value behind the change. Also, make sure that it is purely his choice and not yours. If not, he will rebel.

Deceit

For many years, Ashley and Jared always went to the park each week to have lunch with each other. She consistently brought up how she wanted more time from him and in an effort to please her, he began taking his lunch the same time as Ashley so they could spend more time with each other. Not only did he adjust his schedule but he had given up some other habits to make her happy. He stopped smoking for her months after they met, but soon his habit crept back up on him. Little did Ashley know but Jared used his lunch break to sneak a smoke each day before he came home. But on the days he would meet her for lunch he had to sneak a smoke after work and would just tell Ashley he had to work overtime. Well one day Ashley cancelled lunch with Jared because her coworkers wanted to go out for lunch to celebrate an employee's last day at her company. They decided to get smoothies and go to the park to catch up. It just so happened that it was the same park she and her husband go to when they meet for lunch. Jared was elated Ashley cancelled because he had a stressful day and really needed a smoke to calm his nerves. He decided to still go the park where they usually meet and have a nice smoke break. As Ashley and her friends approached the park, one of her coworkers noticed her husband across the way. Ashley looked and, lo and behold, it was her husband. She commenced to walk over to him, but then, she saw him pull a cigarette out of his pocket, light it up, and have a go! Ashley was astonished. She was so angry but didn't want to show her coworkers and said she would call him when they left the park instead of interrupting his lunch.

Situations like this happen all the time. Spouses change their habits merely to appease their mates when in reality they are simply hiding them. Once again, truly understand why this person has the habit. Share your values behind it and why you just couldn't deal with someone that does whatever habit it may be. Have a real discussion about it and truly hear the other's side. Also, if you see this habit when you start dating, accept it and don't deny the habit. It is there. If this is a habit they want to keep and don't intend to change, then you have to make a choice to accept it or leave. You can't help a person if they don't realize they are sick.

Resentment

When you first met your guy, you praised him for the things you enjoyed about him and decided to mask your true feelings about the things you didn't. You weren't really into how he liked to go fishing every Saturday. You hated when he would wear hats with all of his outfits. You really didn't enjoy going to buffets to eat but you made the best of it and felt that at least he was being resourceful. You had in your mind that you would slowly let him know that you wanted some things to change but at the right time. I mean you should definitely still stay with him because at least he is faithful and loving, right? Now, it is true the man you are supposed to be with will not be perfect. There will be some things that are not there and you need to ask yourself what is more important. But I think some people take this philosophy and apply it to different aspects of the person and the relationship. Yes, it is true that you should value the good in the person but you honestly need to like who they are as a person as well.

Sometimes we will find ourselves falling for a guy because of the way he makes us feel, but not for the person for who he really is. Know the difference. Eventually, you will become annoyed with the things you want changed and will either nag him about the changes or hurt his pride by constantly criticizing him. Either way, your mate will eventually begin to resent you. He will not understand what has changed because you loved him so much at first and for some reason things have changed. But in actuality, nothing has changed. You were just hiding your true feelings. Eventually, this will cause a major discord between you and your mate. He will also resent you because you are trying to change who he is, critiquing who he is, and ultimately not accepting who he is. When you see these traits in the beginning be honest with yourself. It is not fair to yourself, nor is it fair to the person you are with to hide how you truly feel.

Unfair

Rebecca was with Chad for going on three years. Their relationship started off amazingly blissful. They traveled all the time, loved each other's company, and Rebecca truly felt this relationship was going to be it. One day Chad came home acting completely different than usual. Rebecca tried to console him, but his attitude just wouldn't change. Finally Chad told Rebecca that he needed to talk to her and to have a seat. Chad begin to explain to Rebecca that he wasn't happy anymore. He went on to explain why and that he felt Rebecca had changed. He brought up things he just couldn't deal with anymore, that he wasn't in love with her anymore and that he wanted to move out. Rebecca was devastated. She didn't understand how after three years Chad could just fall out of love with her. I read a quote that stated, "No one ever falls out of love with you. Either they were never in love with you or they still are." When I first read it I didn't understand, but then it all made sense. When you really love someone it is unconditional. Regardless of what happens you still love him for who he is. Little did Rebecca know, Chad was never really in love with her. Chad was in love with the idea of being with someone and enjoyed the thrills of always going out and enjoyed the fun they had! As the trips became fewer, and Rebecca became less outgoing, he soon didn't enjoy the relationship anymore. He was in love with the relationship more than he was in love with her.

Can you imagine how that feels? To be in relationship for all that time and he didn't even appreciate who you are? That's what happens when you commit to someone that you know isn't what you are looking for. It's unfair to him. There's someone out there who will love and accept him for exactly who he is and where he is right now. Don't hold him back from that. If you see things in a potential mate, be honest and address it. Also, be okay with the fact that maybe you are just not for each other. That's okay. It's better to be honest now than months later when feelings have gotten involved and promises have been made and cause even more hurt and pain. Let him go so he can find the person that is right for him and so you can as well.

Puppet

Depending on the type of guy you meet, some guys will allow you to change things about them and not say much about it. They will solely do it because they care for you and will do anything to have you in their lives. Usually, guys of this nature are weak-minded and are unsure of themselves and not confident in who they are at the present moment. They are probably still trying to find out who they are and who they want to be and become. So when you come along all confident and know who you are, they think that your suggestions are correct and it is for their good. The issue with this is they will go along with any opinions or thoughts you have because they are unsure and assume you are right. He will become a puppet. Whatever you want to do, he will agree. Whatever you want to change about him, he will do it, though reluctantly. You will become the leader and he will follow willingly.

This is not a healthy relationship by any means. You want a man who can lead and definitely knows who he is. You want someone who balances you and has his own mindset and confidence in who he is. Eventually what will happen is he will continue to change, but one day, it will hit him that this is not who he wants to be. Also, if you can control this weak-minded man, guess what? Anyone else can as well. A man that has a weak mind can be controlled by anyone who can convince him enough that their way is right. He will soon have his strings pulled by another puppet master and you will wonder what has happened to your obedient mate. Stay away from this type of guy. When dating, you need to make sure a guy is mature, knows who he is and is confident in the man God has formed him to be. You want someone who has a vision for himself and a purpose. Ladies remember, you want a man, not a child. You want to be his potential wife, not his potential mother.

These are just a few consequences of ignoring the red flags of a relationship that blatantly show you he is not the one for you. I know you really want to find the one for you and fall madly in love. I get it. But don't make the mistake of just accepting anything and anyone just to have a man. Also, if you are already in a relationship or engaged, realize that your man is who he is and you decided to accept him for exactly who he is today. In all relationships, we have areas to adjust but we can't expect perfection. Unconditional love is loving them for who they are and even accepting their flaws. If you know you love him and know this is the guy for you ask God to help you accept him just as Christ accepts you for who you are. Anyone you date will have some form of annoyances or traits that drive you crazy. That's normal. But when you get in the business of changing people for who they are as far as morals, values, personality, etc., then you need to rethink your intentions. Be patient and let God work on him if it's an issue that could affect you long term. When you first meet a man; observe. If he continues to show you traits that you are just not okay with, then you may want to think about moving on and possibly just being friends. Don't just accept anything so you won't be lonely because eventually you will end up exactly in the place you are fearing; alone.

Chapter 7

Break All Comparisons

Dating can have its ups and downs but, all in all, we learn a lot about ourselves and also dating. After all the dates and mishaps, we can sit back and think of the different guys we have come across, dated, and those we wish we would never have met. Every time we meet one guy we think about the guy we dated before and compare them to each other. This can sometimes be a good thing but it can also be a bad thing. Hopefully, we learn from our past choices that hindered us and we begin to know what signs to look for to ensure we don't make the same mistakes. As soon as a new guy walks into our lives he immediately goes under inspection. Anything we see that reminds us of the past guy that hurt us, cheated on us, lied, or did anything that brought us pain, we freak out and think, "This guy will do the same thing that guy did. I can't trust him." Now the good thing about comparing is that we can learn from our past and adjust the way we handle the present potential guy.

Maybe you learned that you get attached too fast and a past mate exclaimed that you were too needy? You can use this information to work on finding a balance when you are dating a guy and not scare him off. Whatever the comparison may be, we all do it but we have to ensure we are not comparing to the point that you are discouraging the guy's chance of being with you, or to the extent that you can't let go of your past. Many of us fall into the pattern of comparing men unconsciously, and we don't realize; it may sometimes hinder us from being with a great guy. We will miss out on a great catch because we are so busy trying to make him like someone we used to date, or because we are in fear that he is just

LIKE someone we used to date. You have to let that go. Learn from your mistakes from the past. Learn from what you realized about yourself. But do not hold on to past hurts and carry it over to your present relationship. You will place so much on the present guy because of issues that have nothing to do with him. Now if you're lucky, you may find a guy who is patient and understands that you have had a hard past. If he loves you enough he will try to be patient with you as you heal, but its best to heal and let go before you meet your mate.

Some men can't handle that type of pressure because you will find yourself blaming them for issues that are completely irrelevant to them or what they are doing. For instance, let's say you had a guy in the past who used to lie to you a lot and cheated multiple times. You meet a great guy and from day one he is consistent and shows you in many different ways that he is into you and only spends time with you. This consistency goes on for weeks, and then one day you don't hear from the new guy. You usually talk all day and then, out of nowhere, he is absent. You look at the clock passing hour by hour and become more and more upset as it gets later in the evening. Finally you give up on hearing from him and have decided in your mind that he is just like the other guy. Little do you know he has lost his phone and does not know your number by heart. He finally contacts you the next day when he finds his phone but you don't answer. You have made up in your mind that he was with another girl and no matter what excuse he gives you, you will believe he is lying. Now the majority of the time you have known him he has done nothing to make you believe you can't trust him. Every date you have planned, he has been there. Everything he has promised you he will do, he has done. His friends know about you. You know about his friends. He has done everything you can think of to show you that he wants you and only you. However, the one time there is an inconsistency you freak out and revert back to your cocoon of safety because you feel you can't trust him. That's not fair to the new guy at all.

This is why it is so important to have complete healing before entering into a serious courtship with a guy. When you haven't healed from your past relationship, you bring those hurts into the next relationship. When you go into a courtship with a new potential mate start him off with a clean slate. Don't go into it assuming he has a secret vendetta or think he is only trying to play you. Give him a serious chance. If you are going into it with a negative mindset, then you are not ready to date. Save this man the trouble of thinking he even has a chance with you. Now don't misunderstand me, use what you have learned in the past and take note of what you could do differently. Some issues we have had in past relationships are a result of decisions we made, or red flags we ignored. Find the source of the problem and stop blaming men. Sometimes we are the problem. Therefore, changing yourself is the solution. Some believe, "Trust is earned, not given." Some also believe, "Innocent until proven guilty," while others believe "Guilty until proven innocent." Whatever approach you go with, make sure it includes giving him the benefit of the doubt.

There are ways to trust a man but at the same time not to be naïve. If you want to truly find out who a guy is and his intentions, take heed to these tips:

Talk with God right before you go on each date and throughout the courtship.

Every time before I would go on a date with any guy I always prayed to God for spiritual discernment. I wanted to make sure I wasn't focused on the way he dressed, smelled, or the flattering comments he gave. I wanted to see this man the way God did. Ask God for spiritual discernment so you will be guided by your spirit and not your flesh. Usually when we start dating a guy we have our own set agenda in mind and want the relationship to go to the furthest extent possible: marriage. But sometimes that isn't God's plan. While dating, be open to what God's plan is and not your own. Some people we meet may just be for a particular purpose and not the purpose of becoming your husband. Maybe you are supposed to witness to him? Maybe he is there to help you with your next project? Maybe God will use you to send a word? Maybe he just needs a good friend? Find out God's purpose in you all meeting instead of focusing on your own.

When we focus on the guy for the intent of marriage we will ignore red flags and do everything we can to make him fit into our own set dreams and desires instead of God's. We also tend to do this out of desperation and wanting to be with someone so badly that we will take anyone! Don't do that. Truly pray to God about this man that has come into your life and be open to the truth, because God will reveal it to you. Marriage is a serious step and you don't want to rush into anything with anyone just to have someone.

Pay attention to the fruit he is bearing.

Anybody can tell you how they feel about you or sway you with their words. Don't let his mouth speak for him, let his actions speak. If he is a church goer look to see if he exuding qualities of a man that's truly living for Christ. Pay attention to everything he does. His actions will speak volumes.

- Does he exude patience and wisdom?
- Does he use foul language?
- Does he try to keep his temper down?
- Pay attention to his timeliness when you have a date.
- Does he open the door for you?
- Does he tip your waitress at the end of dinner?
- When you are having a conversation do his eyes wander or are they focused on you?
- Does he just go to church, or does he have a true relationship with Christ?
- When you ask him to do something, does he do it or does he always have an excuse?
- Does he pray?
- Does he read his Word?
- Is he respectful of your time?

Galatians 5:22-23 *" But the fruit of the Spirit is love, joy, peace, forbearance, kindness, goodness, faithfulness, gentleness and self-control. Against such things there is no law."*

Keep this scripture in mind when examining your guy. He won't be perfect, and I am sure some of these you need to develop as well. Use this scripture to measure the inner being of your potential mate. Also, check yourself as well to see where you could improve.

Pay attention to how he treats his friends.

Seeing the relationship between a man and his friends will tell you a lot about his character and the things he values in relationships. As the saying goes, "Birds of a feather flock together." Sometimes when you meet guys, they may act as if they are the good guy but the rest of their friends are the players, etc. Or they may try to persuade you that they are nothing like their friends or give excuses for why their friends act the way they do. Sit back and pay close attention to this because he must relate to them in some fashion for him to be their friend. There's something about them that attracted him to that particular crowd and why he wants to be associated with that group. It's also important to ensure he has friends who are Godly men and will steer him in the right direction. When you have an altercation, or he just possibly needs advice, the first place he will go to, hopefully after God, is his friends. Well, if his friends are all single, players, or immature, do you truly think they are going to give him good advice? Do you think they are going to push him to make up with you and do the right thing? Also, single men usually like for their friends to stay exactly that; single. They miss their buddy, and if they don't have good intentions for your potential spouse they will do everything they can to separate you. So get to know his circle. You want to ensure he has a good support system of Godly men that are mature, have wisdom, and if possible, also in relationships or married.

- Are they Godly?
- Do his friends use profanity and he not seem offended?
- What do they do when they go out?
- What type of profession do his friends have?
- Is he loyal to his friends and keeps his word?
- Are they married or in a relationship?
- Are they spiritual?
- Does your potential spouse feel he can depend on them?

Find out about past relationships.

A man's past relationships will say a lot about him as well as what he expects from a relationship. It will also show you how he handles conflict and treats women. It will also show his pattern in relationships.

- Who broke the relationship off?
- Does he admit to the things he did wrong in the relationship or completely blames the woman?
- How long did he date her before he committed?
- How did the relationship end?
- Does he have a similar pattern that seems harmful?

Find out about his family.

This is a BIG one. Family history will tell you a load of information about your potential mate. Home is the first place we see relationships and what we define as normal.

- Did he live in a single parent home?
- Were his parents divorced?
- How close is he to this family?
- Was he the baby of the family, only child, or the oldest?
- Was he the only boy in the family?
- How does his family handle conflict?
- Are they spiritual?

You will be surprised how much family dynamic will tell you about your mate. Ask, ask, and ask. Also, see how the interaction is between his family as well as his interaction with them personally.

Inquire about his goals.

Find out what type of goals he has set for himself financially, professionally, personally, spiritually, mentally, and emotionally.

- Did he meet the goals that he set in the past?
- What is he doing now to meet the current goals he has set?
- Does he seem consistent and disciplined in reaching his goals?
- Are his dreams far-fetched or realistic?
- Is he more of a dreamer or a doer?
- Do his goals match your values?

Pay Attention to Character Traits

When certain situations or confrontations arise pay attention to the way he responds to them.

- How does he respond when someone is angry with him?

- What does he do when his feelings are hurt or pride is hurt?
- Is he moody?
- What does he do when he gets frustrated?
- Does he have control over his emotions?
- How does he handle stress at work?
- Does he tend to victimize himself?
- How does he handle conflict with those he loves?

These are just a few things to pay attention to about your potential mate. Understand that the way he reacts to particular situations will most likely carry over to you all's relationship as well.

What is his relationship with His mother?

So I know you are thinking, "Didn't she just talk about family dynamics?" Yes, I did. But I wanted to separate the mother, because this relationship should be discussed all on its own. The relationship he has with his mother, and also who his mother is as a person, will say a lot about him and what you should expect in your relationship. Men tend to date women who remind them of their mother. Also, the relationship they have with her will define, for some men, what they expect from you. No, they aren't expecting you to mother them, but they may expect the same type of closeness or treatment. Not because he wants his mom, but just because that's how he was treated, or maybe that's how she treated the men of the family. For instance, let's say he and his mother are best friends. They discuss everything with each other and have always had a close bond. Usually every Sunday they eat dinner together and talk about their prior week.

When it comes to you in the relationship, he will probably want the same from you. He definitely doesn't need to be too close to his mother, because he needs to leave to cleave. But he will want to somewhat replace that relationship that he had with her. Also, let's say that the mom usually cooks for him and they rarely go out to dinner as a family. He will most likely like to have home-cooked meals versus going out to eat. Now understand, I am not saying it is your responsibility to be a replica of his mother. That is not your job by any means. I do think though you should definitely understand that his relationship with his mother will transition over to some expectations he has in mind from you. Of course you all can work this out as a couple on what expectations you have from each other and find a balance.

What is his relationship with His father?

A relationship with a man and his father is an important aspect of a man's upbringing as well as his current outlook on marriage, relationships, family, and how he sees the role of the man in the home. Men first learn how to be a man from their fathers, or father figures. He will look to him as an example of how he should treat a woman as well as how he should be in the home. The relationship between his mother and father will be in the forefront of his mind and how he will decide date and treat you. Find out about his father and observe their family dynamic. If a father was absent in the home, this will play a major part in you all's relationship and family. He may be unsure of how to be a husband and father. He may have never seen an example and need guidance on what is right or wrong. Whatever the dynamic may be; ask questions and observe.

- Was his father in his life?
- What is his relationship with his father?
- If he didn't have a father, did he at least have a father figure in his life?
- How does his father treat his mother?
- Does he agree with the way his father handled the home or disagree?
- Was his dad the leader in the home or his mother?
- What is his idea of a father and husband in the home?

Would You Have Him As A Friend?

Going into a relationship with a potential spouse, we tend to speed up the process to get to the romantic side of things instead of building a friendship first. Friendship is the foundation of any successful relationship. When the physical qualities and intimacy go away you need to have something of substance that you want to spend the rest of your life with. Someone that you can genuinely see yourself spending time with and enjoying yourself just as you would a good friend. You want to be able to call him your mate, your best friend, and someone whom you can always depend on. When you look for a good friend, what are the qualities you look for? You should have the same standard for your potential mate.

- Do you all laugh together?
- Is he someone you would be friends with if you weren't even looking for a spouse?
- Can you go to him when you need prayer?
- Is he a loyal friend?
- Is he like-minded?
- Is he dependable?
- Do you feel you can trust him?

Everyone has their idea of what they expect from a friend. Keep in mind the same requirements. You all need to have a solid friendship to have

Chapter 8

Trust God's Timing

Proverbs 19:21 *"Many are the plans in a person's heart, but it is the LORD's purpose that prevails."*

L ife can bring so many ups and downs and many of those ups and downs come from disappointments. Disappointment with where we are in our lives currently. Disappointment with our jobs. Disappointment with our families. All around us, we can find things that remind us that we are not where we want to be or that we don't have the things that we want. We also find ourselves getting disappointed when things don't go our way. We hope. We dream. We aspire to have so much in this life and we already envision exactly how we want it to be. We dream about that perfect job. We dream about that car we have always wanted. We aspire to be better and better than what we are and will sometimes do anything to get there. Not only do we do everything we can, but then we also go to God to ask him for what we desire. We plead for Him to make our dreams come true and most of all, change our present situations. We ask Him when it will come. Why don't I have these things yet? We even find ourselves trying to bargain with God. We all have done this, and we all have in our minds what we want to have and what we want to come into our lives. Along with everything else, I'm sure many of us have asked God to bring us our spouse. And wonder why they have not come into our lives.

"When will he come into my life?"

"Lord, is there something I need to change?"

"Did I already miss him?"

"Why won't you bless me with a spouse?"

"Why is everyone else getting this blessing and not me?"

The questions can go on and on. We do this with the desire of a spouse and things we desire in life, period. But if you notice, many of the things we ask for and desire are what *we* want, and we never think to ask God what *He* desires for us. We have in our minds what we think we want and even think it's what we need. But one thing I have learned is that sometimes what we think we want, we actually don't want it, nor do we need it. We get so consumed with our desires that we never think to ask our Creator what He has in mind. One thing you have to remember is God's ways and thoughts are higher than ours. Also, He created you. Therefore, don't you think He knows what's truly best for you and the best way to fulfill the desires you have?

Isaiah 55:9 *"As the heavens are higher than the earth, so are my ways higher than your ways and my thoughts than your thoughts."*

God is sovereign and all knowing. He was here before you were even thought of and created everything around you. God knows the ins and outs of your needs and desires and he knows the best way and time to fulfill them. We look around at what others have and we find ourselves wondering why we haven't received the same, never understanding what they've been through to get there. What's ironic is that you probably have something that they want. Society does everything it can to make us feel that we need more than what we have and that it's never enough. Every commercial you see is the new car you need to have. The new pair of shoes you need to have. Everything they show is something they put in your mind that you "need" and that what you have now will not suffice. It truly brings on ungratefulness for what God has already blessed us with and makes us begin to idealize the new trend. Society has also made us very impatient. Everywhere you look, you see signs that give you the fast route for fast results and minimum work on your end. Whether it is to lose weight, loan money, or as simple as waiting in line to get an oil change, they have caused us to have very little patience for anything. This lifestyle of quick gratification has sadly transcended into our personal and spiritual lives as well.

We don't want to have patience with people and expect quick change. We also do the same with situations we are in that are a struggle. We want God to change the situation immediately when many times He wants to change YOU in the situation instead. The reason we find ourselves wanting this quick gratification with desires being met, and changes in our situation, is that we hate to be uncomfortable and suffer. As soon as we are uncomfortable in a situation, or having a hard time, we want to get out of the situation as quick as possible and move on to what we think will bring us happiness. When in reality, many times, it's something we are dealing with internally that's really the problem, not the external situation. God knows exactly where we are in every aspect of our lives, and He knows when it is best to move. Understand that God isn't trying to make us happy; He is trying to make us better, to improve us. Just as fire is put to gold to refine it, to purify it, God allows us to go through suffering to purify us, to strengthen our character; to mold us into who He has called us to be.

2 Corinthians 4:17 *"For our light and momentary troubles are achieving for us an eternal glory that far outweighs them all."*

Romans 8:18 *"Consider that our present sufferings are not worth comparing with the glory that will be revealed in us."*

God is molding us to become more and more like Christ, and He loves you so much that He would never keep you from growing into the best you can be. Our suffering, our times of waiting, are all a part of His plan to get us to the end destination He has in mind for us. Not what *we* have in mind, but what *He* has in mind. Sometimes it feels like we are going to wait forever, as if things will never change, but it is only for a season. You are only passing through. It is temporary. Instead of waiting for things to change. Instead of fighting the process. Allow God to work in you.

Here are some steps to take while you are waiting:

- Ask God what He is trying to teach you?
- Look around at what you do have and find the little blessings.
- Write down where you were last year and where you are now. Is there a difference?
- Examine the people God has placed in your life. Is He trying to use you as a blessing to someone else?
- Each morning, ask God for contentment, joy, and acceptance for His plan and not your own. Ask Him to give you strength through your time of struggle.
- Find scriptures that relate to your situation and speak over them.
- Find others who are suffering and help them. Many times when I went through certain situations, I helped others in the same situation and it lifted my spirit.
- Pray daily.
- Journal to God each day about your feelings. He cares for you.
- Each day, write down what you are worrying about for 30 days. After 30 days, look back at the previous days and see what has changed. Are you better than you were 30 days ago?
- Be obedient where He has placed you now.
- Find others to give joy to and watch how quick it changes your mood as well!
- Ask God to give you peace beyond all understanding. But realize that you will have to let go of the need to understand to attain that peace.
- Ask God why you are having a hard time being patient? Ask Him to show you the error of your ways and help you change.
- Learn that it is completely okay to cry and get frustrated sometimes, I've been there. But after you let it out, stop, regroup, pray, and get back to reality.
- Instead of asking why, ask him what He is trying to do in your life.

These are just a few tips to help you get through your journey of waiting. Of course add your own! We all handle situations differently and you have to find what's best for you.

God's Plan

Jeremiah 29:11 *"[11] For I know the plans I have for you," declares the Lord, "plans to prosper you and not to harm you, plans to give you hope and a future."*

Living in such a fast-paced world, we feel the need to catch up to everyone else's life around us. Sometimes it seems that everyone else's life is going according to plan, while yours seems to be at a halt, or nonexistent. We try to figure out what we are doing wrong or when our time will come. We get older and older and become discouraged; thinking that we should be at a certain place in our lives at our age, and become disappointed because we are not. We had our plan worked out perfectly. So what went wrong? Why aren't we there yet? Because it was *our* plan and not *God's*. Sometimes we forget that we are not the author and finisher of our lives; God is. We seem to forget that we don't decide when things happen in our lives; God does. When we get in our minds the timetable of events that should occur in our lives, we begin to push and force those things to happen and it usually ends in destruction. We think we know when it is the best time for us to get married. When it's the best time to get a home. When it's the best time to start a family. But the truth of the matter is, that is completely up to God. Every aspect of our lives is up to God. Now don't get me wrong, I am not saying that you should not plan out certain aspects of your life. But what I am suggesting is to ensure that after you make your plan to surrender it to God and trust His timing. Everyone else's life is not yours and we all receive things when it is right for us. This mindset of feeling we deserve to be a certain place in our lives will cause envy and ungratefulness to grow. What is ironic, is that there is someone looking at you thinking the same thing.

Living in God's plan for our lives is the best kept secret to let peace enter your life. The more and more we try to take control of our lives we become stressed and weary because we are trying to force life to happen instead of letting life happen to us. Think about it like this. When you completely trust someone it's easy to let them handle things. For instance, if you had a spouse who always provided, protected you, and gave you everything you needed right when it was a necessity, you wouldn't question him or worry about being taken care of. You would just get up each day completely at peace, because you know that everything you need will be provided and he is taking care of it. That's how you should think about God. That's exactly what God is doing for you. You don't have to worry about what you will eat tomorrow. You don't have to worry about if you will get this job or that job. You don't have to worry about that project being successful. All you have to do is get up, walk in faith, and be obedient and God will take care of the rest. Many of us walk around so stressed out. You know why? Because we are trying to take care of everything for ourselves. That was never our job. I want you to read this scripture and truly take in what God is trying to convey to us. After you read it, ask yourself, "Why are you worrying?"

> **Matthew 6:25-34** [25] *"Therefore I tell you, do not worry about your life, what you will eat or drink; or about your body, what you will wear. Is not life more than food, and the body more than clothes?* [26] *Look at the birds of the air; they do not sow or reap or store away in barns, and yet your heavenly Father feeds them. Are you not much more valuable than they?* [27] *Can any one of you by worrying add a single hour to your life[a]?* [28] *"And why do you worry about clothes? See how the flowers of the field grow. They do not labor or spin.* [29] *Yet I tell you that not even Solomon in all his splendor was dressed like one of these.* [30] *If that is how God clothes the grass of the field, which is here today and tomorrow is thrown into the fire, will he not much more clothe you—you of little faith?* [31] *So do not worry, saying, 'What shall we eat?' or 'What shall we drink?' or 'What shall we wear?'* [32] *For the pagans run after all these things, and your heavenly Father knows that you need them.* [33] *But seek first his kingdom and his righteousness, and all these things will be given to you as well.* [34] *Therefore do not worry about tomorrow, for tomorrow will worry about itself. Each day has enough trouble of its own."*

So why do we stress about finances? Why do we stress about life, period? Because we simply have forgotten we serve a God who keeps us on His mind always. He thought up the plan for your life before you were even born. God is always thinking about you and has already designed the perfect plan for your life. Which is awesome, because He will always have the best plan for us! So though you may feel you are not where you want to be, know that this is all a part of His perfect plan. That includes even the mistakes you feel you have made. One thing I love about God is that, even when we go off course from His plans, He uses it for our good. One verse that always comforts me when I get off track is *Romans 8:28,*

"²⁸And we know that in all things God works for the good of those who love him, who have been called according to his purpose." It is so comforting to know that anything that happens in our lives, God can turn it for our good. So if you've gone off track a little bit, trying to force things to happen in your life, don't worry. God will use it for your good. I have experienced this for myself. Some of the hardest trials I have gone through, solely because of decisions I made, God allowed me to go through it and it completely changed my mindset on life. Though the struggles have been painful, I wouldn't change a thing because I wouldn't be who I am today. So even if you have made some decisions before you read this, don't feel bad. He is going to work it all out in His plan.

So breathe! Take it easy. Stop trying to figure out when things will come into your life, God has it all under control. Stop looking around feeling you have to compete with the lives of others around you. You don't have to answer to anyone in your life but God. Wherever you are, God has destined you to be there and He is doing a great work in you. Continue to trust Him. He will never disappoint you.

I will admit that it took me years to truly understand the art of accepting and waiting on God. No matter where I was, I was always ready to get to that next job, car, relationship, or anything that would keep me from being in the same place too long. As soon as I would get to one place, I was immediately thinking about the next step. I never wanted to stay in any particular place in my life for too long and would do anything to rush the process. Honestly, until I went through the heartache of being engaged, married, and divorced—in all of 6 months' time—did I learn to stop, be patient, and wait for God. See, that part of my life all happened because of my need to get to a certain place in my life that I "felt" I should have and honestly thought I was ready for.

Sometimes God will allow us to move in the direction we are pushing for in our lives just so we can fall on our faces and realize that we have no earthly idea what we are doing with our lives. Don't make the same mistakes I did. Realize now before things get too hasty to wait for God and accept exactly where He has you know. I promise you He knows what He is doing and knows when it is best to move and change things in your life. After my divorce, my total mindset changed about life. I didn't trust myself anymore. I realized that I didn't know what I truly needed in life, only God did. I learned to be patient and take each day step by step and trust God's process. The more you learn to trust God, be patient, and trust the process He has you in at the moment, your contentment and peace will come. But you have to learn to trust Him. If you really think about it, the reason it's probably so hard for you to wait is that you don't like being uncomfortable. You feel like you should be at a certain place in your life probably either because of your age or because you took certain steps. But if you truly know the God you serve and love, don't you think if you were supposed to be in a certain place in your life, God would have you there?

Acceptance really comes down to how much you trust God. As a Christian, it isn't just about knowing God and believing in His word, but about giving TOTAL control over to him. When you learn to give over the control of your life to God, there is so much freedom. I truly found this out after my divorce. Before my divorce, I rushed everything. I always had to know what was happening in my life and had to have control over everything. God allowed me to have control of my life and I got everything I planned on getting, and it turned into a disaster. As much as it hurt, God had to allow me to go through the turmoil so I could get out of my own way. God knew that I would continue to insist on my plan being done and not be open to what He had planned for me. After everything I truly learned to let God know my desires and sit back patiently and trust He will provide where is needed, and He hasn't failed me yet by any means.

Learn to trust God totally in your life. I mean in *truly* every aspect of your life each and every day. Want a new job? Ask and Trust God. Want your own place? Ask and Trust God. Want to learn to get out of debt? Ask and trust God. Need new friends? Ask and trust God. Whatever it is that you need or even desire just ask and trust God and wait. There is so much peace that comes over you when you get in a place of rest about your life. There is nothing like it.

Ecclesiastes 3:11 *"To everything there is a season, and a time to every purpose under the heaven"*

Everything in our lives that occurs has a proper place and timing, and God knows exactly when to have things move in your life all the way to the hour, minute, and second. He knows exactly when it will happen, who it will happen through, where, and even how you will react. What is so great about God is that He usually will bring those desires in your life and adds what I like to call a couple of sprinkles on top. He will not only give you your desires, but He adds a little extra surprise when it appears. It's such a great feeling because it is an awesome reminder that God goes beyond just being your provider and keeper, but a sweet, loving spirit that genuinely enjoys blessing His children and putting a smile on our faces. I'm telling you, God is the best thing that will ever happen in your life and will show you a love you have never experienced. How can you not trust a God like that?

Matthew 7:11 *"If ye then, being evil, know how to give good gifts unto your children, how much more shall your Father which is in heaven give good things to them that ask him?*

Ephesians 3:20 *"Now to him who is able to do far more abundantly than all that we ask or think, according to the power at work within us."*

Chapter 9

The Ultimate Love Affair

Being in love is such a great gift that God has given us. It is natural for us to want companionship and God completely understands that. It is somewhat a void within us that needs others around for support, intimacy, friendship, and so much more. From the beginning of time, God saw this need in Adam and provided companionship for him through Eve. He had blessed him with everything on earth and had animals surrounding him, but it just didn't fit the mold like the existence of another human being just like him. God saw this need and provided for Adam his support.

Genesis 2:18-24 *[18] The LORD God said, "It is not good for the man to be alone. I will make a helper suitable for him." [19] Now the LORD God had formed out of the ground all the wild animals and all the birds in the sky. He brought them to the man to see what he would name them; and whatever the man called each living creature, that was its name. [20] So the man gave names to all the livestock, the birds in the sky and all the wild animals. But for Adam[f] no suitable helper was found. [21] So the LORD God caused the man to fall into a deep sleep; and while he was sleeping, he took one of the man's ribs[g] and then closed up the place with flesh. [22] Then the LORD God made a woman from the rib[h] he had taken out of the man, and he brought her to the man. [23] The man said, "This is now bone of my bones and flesh of my flesh; she shall be called 'woman,' for she was taken out of man." [24] That is why a man leaves his father and mother and is united to his wife, and they become one flesh.*

It is so a beautiful when two people come together as one under God. Nothing like having continued support from someone who has committed his life to you and decide to start a new life and family. God loves this union and blesses the act of marriage. Adam and Eve were the first marriage and God saw Eve as a helpmate to Adam and vice versa. Though he blessed Adam with Eve due to his feeling of loneliness, notice that He calls Eve his helpmate. They become one flesh, but He never says that this woman completes the man but only supports and complements. They become one, but one and complete *in* Christ. The reason I want you to notice this is because, though He provided Adam with Eve, He never created her to replace God but merely support Adam. We look to companionship to complete us when God ordained it to support us. That if we don't have this companionship, we can't go on with our lives and are missing an important part of our being. But God never says this. God doesn't want any man or woman to take His place in your heart. Anything He gives us is merely a blessing, a supplemental part of our life. But do not confuse your blessing with your all-in-all.

God is your all-in-all. God never wants you to forget that, and sometimes this is why He waits to provide us with a spouse. He wants to make sure that you understand that He is your everything, not a man. Understanding this concept will also help you to not put so much pressure and expectation in your spouse. He cannot be and do everything for you. God still wants you to come to Him for your needs. He still wants you to cry out to Him. He still wants you to depend on Him to provide for you. He still wants to be the first one you call when you need answers or support. Always remember that. When I dated, one thing I noticed immediately was that my time with God seemed to dwindle. Before I was distracted with a relationship, I was constantly talking to God through journaling, prayer, or worship. God was my main man! Then, as soon as a male came around, I noticed that all of my attention went to him. Now don't feel bad about this if you have done this. It is somewhat normal for our cares to begin going to the male around us. It is natural. So natural, that Paul discusses this conflict in Corinthians.

1 Corinthians 7:32-35 *"32 I would like you to be free from concern. An unmarried man is concerned about the Lord's* *affairs—how he can please the Lord. ³³ But a married man is concerned about the affairs of this world—how he can please his wife— ³⁴ and his interests are divided. An unmarried woman or virgin is concerned about the Lord's affairs: Her aim is to be devoted to the Lord in both body and spirit. But a married woman is concerned about the affairs of this world—how she can please her husband. ³⁵ I am saying this for your own good, not to restrict you, but that you may live in a right way in undivided devotion to the Lord."*

When we are devoted to a spouse it's normal for us to be concerned about their desires and wants. We want to make them happy and try our best to be the spouse they need and have always desired. Our interests turn to them and our families and we can sometimes disregard God unconsciously. This is why Paul brings up the blessing in being single as well because you are only devoted to God. Valuing your relationship you have with God now is so important while being single instead of constantly wishing for a spouse to come into your life.

Your relationship with God is truly like a sweet, unending love affair. While you are single, treat God just as you would a spouse. The calls, the conversations, the quality time you plan, everything you would do with your mate, do it with God. People tend to detach God from their lives as if He doesn't want that love and devotion just as a person on Earth. He wants such a close relationship with you, and He is just waiting on you with open arms. Your relationship with God should mirror your desires for a mate and will help you be a better help mate to your future spouse. For you to truly be a loving spouse, the way God desires, a relationship with God will mold you perfectly for companionship.

God wants all of your attention. He wants you to seek His love, His will, and His protection and guidance above anyone else. Instead of focusing on what you want out of life, focus on God. The rest will be added to you. He wants you to delight in His presence. Delight in getting to know Him and spending time with Him. He wants to know that there is nothing or no one that's more important to you than Him.

Matthew 6:33 *But seek first the kingdom of God and His righteousness, and all these things shall be added to you.*

Psalm 37:4 *"Delight yourself in the Lord, and He will give you the desires of your heart."*

So what exactly is delighting yourself in the Lord? What exactly does it mean to seek God first? When I first read these verses, I didn't quite understand how to do this or what it meant. I thought it meant that I just need to follow his commandments and seek His will and His way. But it means so much more than that. He truly wants you to be focused solely on Him. Do you feel your relationship with God is close or just a Sunday type of relationship? Do you truly see and call on God like a father and best friend? A relationship with God will be the first relationship that will give you the true meaning of love. Here are some steps to take to deepen your relationship with God. Experiencing a relationship with God is one that is beyond unexplainable. You will experience love in a way that is full and complete. Go through these steps to get to know Him, it will be beyond worth it.

- **Communicate with God Daily**

Whether that's through journaling, singing, or praying, ensure to always talk to Him. This doesn't have to be formal, nor does it have to what you "think" you need to say. God wants you to speak with Him openly and honestly. I mean why not? He knows what's on your heart anyways. Remember; treat God just like you would if you met a new potential mate in your life. Remember how you want to talk to them all the time, whether it's on a date, texting, or anything! Be just as anxious to get to know God. Only difference is, the love being returned is guaranteed.

- **Pray Always**

Though this is a part of communicating with God, I wanted to separate this one because it is SO vital. Praying each day is not only communication with your Father and best friend, but it is a way of showing honor to God as well because you are acknowledging that you need Him and letting Him direct your day instead of yourself. It is also a reminder for you that you are not in this life alone. That you have a helper, comforter, and friend. I have always noticed a difference in my day when I haven't spoken with God. I focus more on what is around me and let my circumstances affect my faith and behavior. Praying to God helps to remind you that God is in control of your life and that you can depend on Him through it all. It is a reminder to focus on Him and not your problems.

• Intentionally Set Time Apart for God

Many times we go throughout the day and we get to God only if we have time. We don't see it as being important and we treat it as if it is something to check off on a to-do list instead of making it a priority. I remember my pastor saying "If He isn't number one on the priority list, then He isn't a priority." God should be the first thing on your list, not the second, third, fourth, or fifth. Not Facebook. Not Twitter. Not Instagram. But God. I am only able to tell you this because I did it as well. One day I noticed that, as soon as I woke up, the first thing I did was reach for my phone. I would check my email, Facebook, Twitter, and Instagram. One morning, I just didn't feel right about it. I felt convicted and I quickly realized, I shouldn't be reaching for my phone first thing in the morning, I should be reaching for my Bible. Make time for God. Find out when it's the best time for you to truly get away with some quiet, intimate time with Him. For me, I have to wake up an hour or so early before I get up to prepare for my day. Everyone is asleep. It is total silence and I don't have to worry about getting interrupted. Find the best time for you.

• Read Your Bible

We hear this all the time. I remember people telling me in church all the time to read the Bible, read the Bible, and read the Bible again. It gets to a point where you turn a deaf ear to it. But as I got older, I soon realized just how important this is. Your Bible is the key to getting to know God and having a better life. It is so much in the Word. Every situation you are going through, there is a passage about it or a person in the Bible who has gone through it. The Bible also helps you to get to know who God is. Sometimes, I would find myself falling in love with God from reading all the things He had done for others and it would remind me that He would do the same for me. It made God real for me when I saw Him showing compassion, grace, love, and forgiveness towards His children. That's what's so amazing about God. Not only can you talk to Him, but you can read about Him to get to know Him better. The great thing now in this generation is that we have so many accessible resources to read the Bible that we truly have no excuse to not read it. We have Bible apps for our phones and devices. A million plans to help guide you in your reading. A ton of different versions so you can understand the Bible beyond the King James Version. Not only that, you can have audio for it to be read to you. There truly isn't an excuse. But I will tell you this. Don't do it out of obligation, but do it out of love for your Father. Just try it. The more you read the more you will want to read. The more you read, the more you will fall in love with Him. I promise, you won't regret it.

• Praise & Worship

You can worship God through giving, showing love, and using your gifts for Him. Praise is an amazing way to show your love for Him. Just like when you have a spouse, you find out what they love and what makes them happy and you do it. The same goes for God. Find out what He loves, what makes Him happy and walk it out. This will bring so much joy to God. Not just at church, but even in your time with God. Praise and Worship is your way of honoring God, but it also distracts you from any problems in your life. See it as singing a love song to God. Your spirit will be lifted. It will also put the words you are singing into your heart and give you peace. Also, realize that praise and worship is beyond singing. You can praise God in your giving, service, and other gifts. Praise will increase your relationship with Christ.

• Go to God Instead of Man

Being on Earth, and in the flesh, it is natural for us to reach out for people and things around us for comfort, support, and to fill voids we have day to day. When we are hungry, we eat. When we need someone to talk to, we go to a counselor or best friend. When we are sad, we automatically find something to distract our minds to bring happiness. Whatever the feeling, whatever the void, we try to find what we can to get a quick relief. But does it truly fulfill what we need? Have you noticed that, usually, when we go to the things around us, it satisfies the need for the moment, but the feeling soon comes back unexpectedly?

This happens because you are *in* this world, but you are not *of* it. Many of the feelings we have and feel are internal and we are reaching for the external to take care of it. The only person, the only thing that can truly fulfill you and help you in any situation, is God.

Now understand, I am not trying to say it is wrong to talk to others for advice or support. Even the Bible recommends Godly counsel. But what I am saying is, don't *depend* on it, or people, to be able to do the complete work of what you need, only God can do that. This will also help you in your relationships because you won't run to your husband to fulfill every need that arises. This also helps with preventing addiction to attention, food, or any other external source to fulfill an internal need. When you learn to go to God to take care of you, you will soon find He can truly be your everything.

God is always there waiting for us to come to Him. Actually, that's exactly what He desires the most from us. So while you are single, learn now to go to God about everything. That way when you are married and you are having trouble with your spouse, you'll go to God. When you have trouble with your children, go to God. When you can't figure out how you all will make the bills for next month, go to God. If you are having trouble conceiving a child, go to God. He has all you need and can provide for you better than any person or thing. He ALWAYS comes through.

• Give It To God

Putting your dependence on God instead of man can be a hard transition for many of us, particularly as women. Whatever role we play at the moment, it's natural for us to take control and handle every situation that comes into our lives. As soon as things go into disarray we find ourselves jumping at the first choice to handle the problem for ourselves. We find the money to pay the bill. We take full responsibility to fix our sibling's issues. We take in the family member that is sick and needs support. We call the plumber as soon as we see the leak in the faucet. Without haste, we try our best to fix the problem immediately because if we don't, no one else will! Or that's what we think at least. It's hard for us to stop, think, and ask God to give us direction on how to handle the situation because, sadly, we have come to trust ourselves more than we trust God.

But how did we get here? When did it get to the point that we must take matters into our own hands instead of trusting the One that has all of the answers and power to fix our issues way better than we ever could? When you really sit back and think about the first initial feeling you have when problems arise, you will immediately recognize that you are moving out of fear: Fear that things will get worse if you don't fix it immediately; or fear that God will take too long, and obviously doesn't understand the importance of timing. We fear that God won't take care of us. We go by impulse when things arise instead of stopping, sitting back, and remembering who is in control: God. We take on control in our lives because honestly we think that God is not in control. We think that if we don't take care of this problem immediately, that everything will become worse and we will not survive. Think of a time that you had a problem arise in your life. Did you go into fear and handled it immediately? Or did you stop, pray, and ask God for direction? I am sure many of us have done the former.

Ultimately, your relationship with God will hold you in every situation and relationship in your life. True fulfilment in all your areas of emptiness will come through Christ. Get to know your maker. He is in love with you and desires a close, intimate relationship with you. Everything you've been missing can be found in Him.

About the Author

Chloe M. Gooden is a mentor, speaker, and author of *Not Tonight: My Worth Is Far Above Rubies*. She has spoken at events on the life of celibacy, sexual temptation, dating, and relationships. She is the creator and manager of Her Worth Is Far Above Rubies, a community which is focused on encouraging women who are celibate, single, brokenhearted, and divorced. She is from Birmingham, Alabama and graduated from Mississippi State University for her Bachelors and University of Alabama at Birmingham for her Masters. She is to attend Central Baptist Theological Seminary to pursue her Master's Degree in Divinity in Nashville, Tennessee this Fall. Her passion is to encourage and enlighten others through God's Word. She hopes to continue helping others to develop an intimate relationship with Christ.

CONNECT WITH US

Chloe M. Gooden
Facebook: Chloe M. Gooden
Instagram: @chloemgooden
Twitter: @chloemgooden

Her Worth is Far Above Rubies
Facebook: Her Worth Is Far Above Rubies
Instagram: @knowyourworthrubies
Twitter: @AboveRubiesUR

THANKS FOR READING!

WE INVITE YOU TO SHARE YOUR THOUGHTS AND REACTIONS!

Other Books by Chloe M. Gooden

Single to Married Devotional
30 Days of Transformation, Restoration, and Healing

Get the perfect companion guide to Single to Married and be guided in prayer and reflection. Helping you transform in being whole in Christ!

Single to Married Devotional gives you a 30 day prayer starter and reflection to help you work through emotional, relational, and spiritual battles and hardships. This devotional is the perfect companion to your Single to Married reading to help you become the woman that God formed you to be: Healed, Transformed, and Restored.

Not Tonight
My Worth Is Far Above Rubies

Struggling in the Life of Celibacy?
Finding It Hard to Fight Sexual Temptation?

Not Tonight guides you through your journey of Celibacy, Sexual Addictions, and Temptation. This book will give you biblical insight, dating tips, and instruction to help you remain pure in your walk. This is a much needed eye opener to any Adult, Young Adult and Teen who is single, dating, or in a relationship.

70087504R00064

Made in the USA
Lexington, KY
08 November 2017